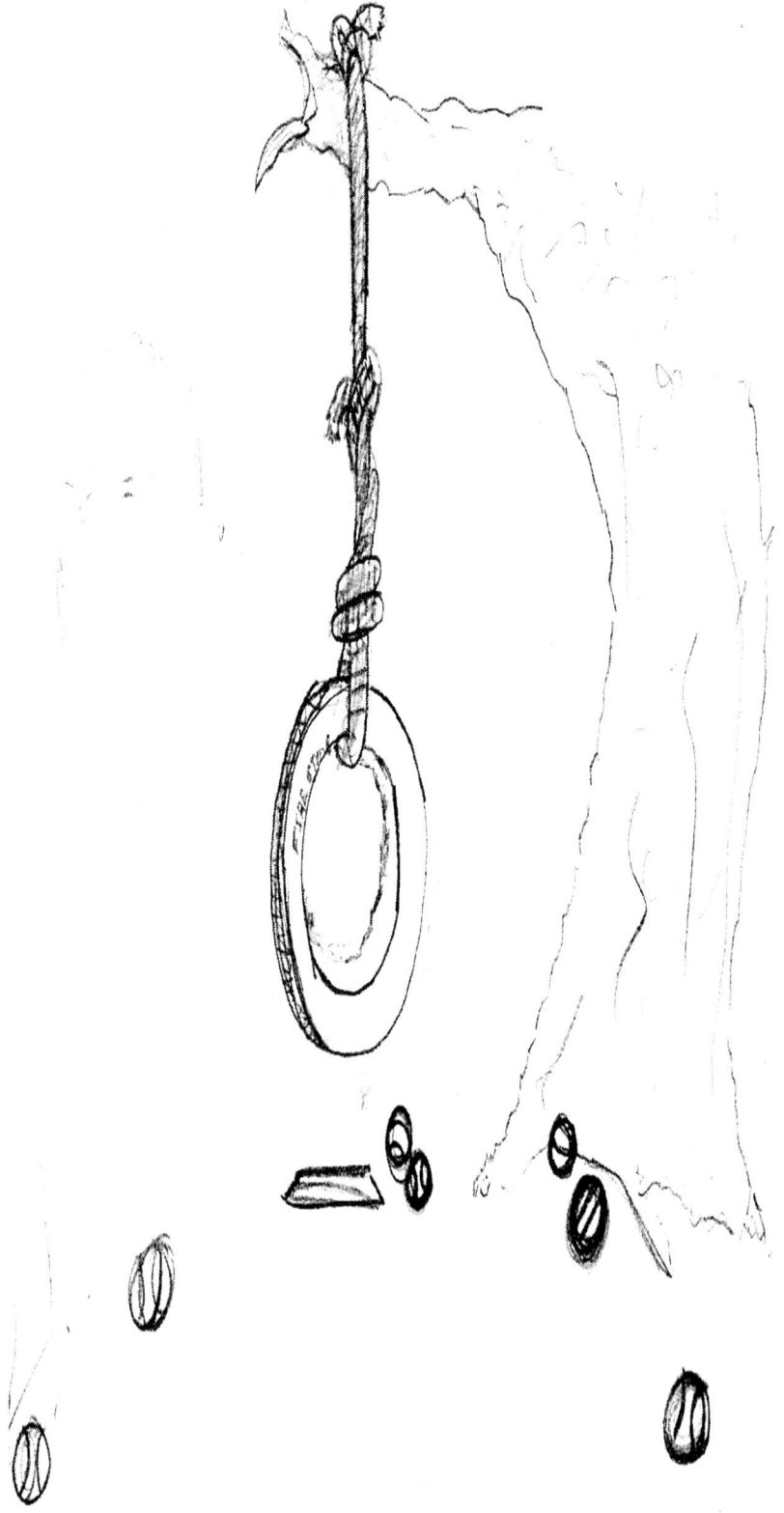

PHANTOM OF THE BULLPEN

ALLEN WHITE

ISBN: 978-1-66784-139-7 (print)

ISBN 978-1-66784-140-3 (eBook)

Prologue

October 4, 1991, 7:15pm
Durham Athletic Park
Durham, North Carolina

Earlier in the day, some poor guy had done his best to draw an on-deck circle, but in his haste had instead created an asymmetrical pentagram. I'd seen worse, though, for sure. I had actually done worse myself, as a coach in a hurry, trying to get a field ready for a game. Ugly, lopsided things, not worthy of remembering, but just good enough to keep some kid from getting his head knocked off by a screaming foul ball. I think the first one I ever drew was large enough to be seen from space.

Houston, we have a prob– What the hell is *that?*

But what if this one *wasn't* an apparent rush job and had some sort of hidden meaning? I was suddenly scared to get in it.

We had beaten up on the Wake Forest Dodgers rather badly a few times before, but that's no reason for them to break out the voodoo stuff. It's not our fault most of their games were mercifully called after five innings because they'd been slaughtered 15-3 or 18-2 and bled Dodger blue all over the field. I counted five little uneven piles of lime in that devil's halo, confirming that the guy had done it by hand, and possibly on purpose.

The early autumn evening still held the South's late-summer humidity and my hands were starting to feel clammy. I had never owned a batting glove, so I stepped down into the dugout and scooped up some exceptionally fine and dry dirt from underneath the bench, which is the best place on earth for mining this valuable commodity. Climbing back out onto the field, I was not looking forward to standing in that – that *thing* to take my warm-up cuts. I grabbed my Brooks Robinson-autographed Louisville Slugger and rubbed some of my magic dirt up and down the handle and all over my hands; works every time and doesn't cost a dime. The little bit I had left over I tossed down the gullet of the jagged gaping maw and stood well to the side of that looming white omen.

Like I said, it was a muggy Friday night, the first weekend in October and I found myself, at age 36, still playing baseball. All those Michelob ads were wrong; it doesn't get any better than this. From the stadium's PA system, I could hear John Fogerty begging his coach to put him in, but I didn't need to hear a song to get pumped. I was plenty pumped already. This was my first game ever at the historic downtown Durham ballpark.

Squeezing and grinding my bat in my customary death grip, I tried to study the Dodger pitcher. I batted fifth in the lineup behind Stacy Overman who, more often than not, cleaned the bases like he's supposed to, leaving me with few opportunities for an RBI. I wasn't stat crazy, but everybody likes to get a ribbie every now and then.

Sure enough, with runners on the corners and one out, Stacy, a lefty like me, crushed the first pitch he saw over the right field fence, way the hell over the bull standing on an ad thirty feet above the fence, and onto the roof of one of Durham, North Carolina's finer cigarette factories. Good. Just in time. That weird on-deck anti-circle thing was beginning to really freak me out. I'm not superstitious like a lot of baseball ballplayers, but I don't take any unnecessary chances either.

Stacy rounded the bases with ease, tipping his batting helmet to the sparse crowd. Flashing a slightly slanted Clark Gable smile and sporting a modified pencil-thin moustache, he hopped on home plate with both feet and blew his wife a kiss. When he floated by me on his way to the dugout, I gave Stacey a high-five, a low-five, and then handed him my cigarette. I said, "Hold this. I'll be right back."

The rightfield corner of historic Durham Athletic Park. It's 305' down the line. The Bulls now have a new and more modern facility a few blocks away, but the old park is still used for special events these days. Stacey Overman's homer landed on top of the building behind the Smoking Bull.

I stepped into the batter's box and assumed my unassuming open stance, leaned back with my bat on my shoulder, and stared down the pitcher. My stance was so open, in fact, it may have looked as though I already had one foot in the bucket, as if I might not even like to hit, or was scared to hit. Au contraire. Nothing could be further from the truth. I always thought everyone played baseball solely for the purpose of getting a few chances to knock the cover off the damn thing. I know I did. The best lesson I ever learned about hitting was not to see how *far* I could hit it, but to see how *hard* I could hit it.

I took a deep breath and let it out slowly, checked the trademark on my bat, dug in, and looked out again to the mound at the lanky Dodger pitcher.

What a letdown.

Just another frustrated jock trying to relive his glory days.

Sorry, pal. So am I.

The guy was tall enough, 6'3" or so, with ears that stuck out like a Yellow Cab with the back doors flung wide open. I almost snickered, but, as a rule, guys with a slight overbite like mine don't laugh at other people's physical abnormalities. Ok. Sometimes we do. Maybe I snickered a little bit anyway; he was probably snickering at me, too.

He appeared to be a little younger than me, maybe, but he looked kind of frail, too. One thing I'm not, at 6-feet even and 220, is frail. This cat's already down three-zip with only one out in the top of the first, and I guessed his confidence level might have been running a little low right about then. His eyes had already gone from 'deer in the headlights' big to 'deer coming through the windshield' huge.

He threw me two pitches that were way outside before he got one close enough for me to hit. A 75-mile per hour fastball is an oxymoron, but that's what he threw, and this one was right on the inside corner and about belt-high. A lefty hitter's dream: something you can turn on. And I turned on it.

The ball jumped off my bat, cleared the right field fence in no time, and just barely missed tearing off one of the famous smoking bull's big horns. A sign on the bull read: HIT BULL, WIN STEAK DINNER! With my near miss, I figured I was still looking at Mickey D's, a quarter-pounder with cheese, and yes, I'll want 'fries wid dat' on the way home.

I rounded the bases in a trance because I'd never hit a lot of homeruns. Perhaps ten or so in Little League and Pony League, and another four or five in high school, and two of those didn't even make it over the fence. They somehow got lost in the honeysuckle vines that covered the fence in the out-field at my school. Thank the Lord for home field advantage.

But somehow, I knew I was going to hit that one. I knew it the second I handed Stacy my cigarette.

When I descended the dugout steps, Stacy fived me and handed me back my smoke. He said, "Callin' your shots now, White?"

Embarrassed and elated by the passing (and not to mention ridiculous) comparison to the Babe, I asked, "Did Ruth ever play here?" I sat down beside my friend and tried to breathe normally. The cigarette didn't help.

Stacy stuffed a handful of sunflower seeds into his mouth. One stuck to his chin; another to his top lip. He got most of them situated, puffed out his cheeks and, in a sudden burst of air, replied, "Probably."

The one from his lip whizzed by the end of my nose and landed harmlessly inside an open pack of Beechnut chewing tobacco. The one on his chin held on for a second or two longer and then dropped into the nearly-empty Gatorade bottle he was holding between his legs. I said nothing. He continued, "A lot of 'em did: Yaz, Hammerin' Hank, Stan the Man, Joe Morgan, Eddie Matthews." He took a swig from his Gatorade, swallowed hard, grimaced, and said with a definite catch in his voice, "There are a lot of memories here; a thousand stories."

"A thousand stories," I echoed.

Little did I know that, just around the corner, the next story waited patiently, silently for me.

The Zebulon Pirates team that beat the Dodgers on a hot, muggy Friday night a week before the Bull Durham Mini World Series: Back row (l-r) Todd Pearce, Mac McDaniel, Stanley 'No Show' Jones, Kirk Pollard, Randy Pearce, Walt Perry. Front row (l-r) Allen White, Welton Pearce, Ricky Strickland, Stacey Overman, Roger Woods, Tim Dahlke. (Ricky and Stacy missed the memo on which shirt to wear.)

Chapter 1

IN THE SPRING OF 1991, I founded the Zebulon Pirates Baseball Club. At age 36, I still had (and still do, at age 67) a burning desire to saw off a guy's bat just above his hands with hard, inside heat or tie him in a knot with a wicked off-speed curveball. I still wanted to rip doubles to the opposite field gap and run the bases like I never could. I still yearned to use my spikes to walk up the wall in left at a dead run and snag somebody's almost-homerun just above the top of the fence and generally raise Cain with other guys sharing similar interests.

The result of all this selfishness became the Zebulon Pirates, a motley crew of washed-up has-beens determined to stay young forever. Selfish is simply the best word to describe a guy harboring these adolescent desires at such a mature age, considering the cost of chasing this constant, but elusive dream. Considering the lost family time, missing a day of work here and there, and all the aches and pains, I had to wonder sometimes if it was really worth it.

All of us, at one time or another, had broken, fractured, or dislocated at least half of the bones in our extremities and pulled, torn, strained, sprained or hyperextended every major muscle in our bodies. Toss in some serious bruises thanks to some bad hops and even worse pitches, and the unspoken question was never far from our thoughts. *Why?*

But did we really care? Hell, no. We're playing baseball!

We competed in the Men's Senior Baseball League's over-30 division. The over-30 league is for guys who are not quite over-the-hill yet, just merely stalled out on the way up. I've been playing or coaching baseball since I was eight years old and that gives me more than fifty years of experience with the national pastime. I know a little bit about the game, and I hope that gives some credence to this true story.

In the summer of 1991, a baseball stadium was built in the middle of a tobacco field one mile from our town limits for the Carolina Mudcats, the AA affiliate of the Pittsburgh Pirates. Zebulon is a classic small town twenty miles east of Raleigh, North Carolina, the state capital. It's a small town just like thousands of small towns across America: three strip malls, two traffic lights, one weekly newspaper, and a partridge in a pine tree. Zebulon, however, has the unique distinction of sitting right smack dab in the middle of God's Country.

I realize that's a strong statement, but it's true, nonetheless. North Carolina State University, the University of North Carolina at Chapel Hill, East Carolina University and Duke University are all within an hour's drive. Travel a few hours west on I-40 to the Blue Ridge Parkway and you're in the Appalachian Mountains. Cruise a few hours east on US-64 to Cape Hatteras or Kitty Hawk and you're on the Outer Banks looking across the Atlantic Ocean. And now there's professional baseball in my backyard?

Like I said, God's Country.

Affectionately dubbed as "Our Field of Dreams" at the ritual groundbreaking ceremony, beautiful and spacious Five County Stadium was completed just in time for a Fourth of July premiere. On opening night, a five-gallon bucket full of dirt – fresh from the farm in Dyersville, Iowa where the hit movie "Field of Dreams" came to life a few years earlier – was spread out all around the pitcher's mound and at home plate by team owner Steve Bryant and some other dignitaries. A profoundly moving and emotional celebration followed. I can still see the colorful fireworks exploding against the backdrop of a black velvet starry sky and hear the oos and ahs from the 8,000-plus fans still in attendance after the game was over that first night.

Three months later, at close to 2 in the afternoon on Sunday, October 13, my team was in Durham, preparing to take on the Durham-Raleigh Twins for the championship of the First Annual 'Bull Durham' Mini World Series at historic Durham Athletic Park. The DAP was the home of the

Durham Bulls, the Class A farm team of the Atlanta Braves and also one of the locations where the hit movie "Bull Durham" was filmed some years before.

We were 1-0 at the DAP in our inaugural year. We had massacred the Dodgers there nine days earlier and then defeated two other teams in Raleigh the day before to make it to the championship game.

With all the Hollywood connections and the history thing nipping at us from behind, Kevin Costner was our obvious number one choice to throw out the traditional first pitch, but it was twenty-five minutes to game time and we lacked the necessary pull to get him there anyway. We settled for our second pick, Kevin Jones, the hotdog man from the concession stand. He did just fine.

We were in the middle of our pre-game warm-ups when I noticed an elderly gentleman weaving his way through the fifty or so fans in the stands and gingerly making his way down to the field. The closer he came, the deeper he fell into my stereotyped category of homeless wino. He looked to be in his late sixties, had on way too many clothes for the eighty-degree temperature, and worst of all, he was heading straight for me. The gray stubble on his chin told me he hadn't shaved in several days and his hair was kind of shaggy, but hey, so was mine. It was his eyes that didn't seem to make contact with anything for more than a second or two that told me all I wanted to know about *this* character.

"Here we go again," I sighed to left fielder Randy Pearce who was also tracking him. Randy and I had played ball with and against each other for twenty years. We knew that a ballfield could sometimes attract a strange clientele. Hell, look at us.

Randy answered, "Nope. Here *you* go again," his voice trailing away as he followed a sudden urge to run wind sprints in the opposite direction.

The old fellow had made it down to the gate beside the dugout and leaned over it. "You the manager?" he asked, looking mostly at me.

"Why me?" I whispered over my shoulder to Walt Perry, our third baseman, who said nothing, but made an equally hasty exit from the scene.

Maybe if I ignore him, he'll just go away, I thought.

"SCUSE ME! ARE YOU THE MANAGER?" the man repeated loudly in my general direction.

So much for that 'thinking' shit. I should know better by now.

Blessed at the time with 20/20 vision and seeing no easy way out, I answered, "I'm close enough, I guess. What can I do for ya?"

"You reckon I could throw you a couple?" he asked shyly, showing me three extremely weathered baseballs and an old, beat up-looking glove.

I could feel myself giving in, but I tried hard to recover. Glancing over my shoulder, I noticed the Twins were already taking some infield practice. "Out on the field?" I returned his question with a question hoping his answer would be, 'Ah, just forget it.'

"Oh, no," he bellowed, pointing due north. "Down there in the bullpen!"

What was I thinking? It's local public knowledge that I have no luck whatsoever. I'm always the guy in line *behind* the proverbial one millionth customer. In fact, the only time opportunity *did* come knocking at my front door, I was out in the backyard looking for four-leaf clovers.

Right on cue, my head started shaking from side to side because I'd gotten myself in situations like this many times before. It comes from the distressing inability to say 'NO!' when it's obviously the right thing to say. Long ago one of my close friends informed me that he had finally arranged to get a date with the girl of his dreams if, and only if, I would agree to a double-date with her friend, who was NOT the girl of my dreams. All I had to do was say 'NO!' but I couldn't do it then and I couldn't do it now.

I should have explained to this old man that *I* haven't finished my stretching yet and *I* need to throw some *myself* and the game starts in about *fifteen* minutes, but then I realized that he and I could be finished throwing a few by the time I explained all that stuff to him.

"Sure, c'mon," I mumbled, trying not to look as bothered by the situation as I really was.

Please don't get me wrong here. I have always had the utmost respect for old people. In fact, one of my main goals in life is to keep growing older. The late Richard Pryor once said, "You don't get old bein' no fool." Even though Mr. Pryor and countless others, including yours truly, have proved that there are some exceptions to that rule, I didn't think this old dude was a fool.

But I've been fooled before and nobody wants to be the last link in a *Chain of Fools.*

As we walked down the third base line toward the visiting team's bullpen and out into foul territory by the left field bleachers, I kicked myself in the butt every other step for not saying 'NO!' when I had the chance. All the way out there I was thinking *"this old-timer's gonna have me chasing balls all over left field and I'm gonna be worn out by the time I take the mound in what - twelve minutes?"* I almost hollered for our catcher, Jim Young, to come babysit for the guy. Then I remembered something my grandmother told me long ago: If you make the bed, you have to lie in it.

Gee. Thanks, Grandma. And thanks for the one warning me that "If you lie down with the dogs, you're gonna get up with the fleas." That one I had to experience both figuratively and literally (yes, a couple of times) before I understood.

I kept walking past the dual mounds to the double plates and got behind the one closest to the foul line. When I turned around, I saw the winner of the Will Geer look-a-like contest climbing the mound next to the fence and the cheap seats. Will Geer? Grandpa Walton on *The Walton's* television show? Never mind. Google him and see for yourself.

"That's just great," I said a lot louder than I meant to. "It's gonna take us ten minutes just to get *set up* so I can chase baseballs."

I looked down at the ground, sort of disgusted, kicked some dirt, and stepped over to the other plate. When I peered up again, *he* was looking down at the ground, kicking dirt, obviously disgusted as well, and moved over to the other mound! I then looked up to that clear Carolina blue sky for help when something or someone softly said, "*Be patient.*"

Instantly I thought, *"Now what in the Field of Dreams crazy bullshit kind of nonsense is this?"* But, on the other hand, I had never heard a voice from Nowhere like that before, so I got patient – really quick.

Inside (I hope), I shuddered when I thought about who might be the owner of that voice. Was it my inner if not deeper self? Did I even have such a thing? I doubted it. Could it have been this old man's guardian angel? Was it God Himself? I shuddered again, on outside this time, for sure. There was no one else within 60'6" of me, so I figured it was just me having a fleeting thought, however unlikely that was.

After one more little two-step with my wino friend, we finally got lined up on the same mound and plate. I felt somewhat relieved, but the relief didn't last very long at all.

The dreamlike series of events that transpired during the next eight to ten minutes unfolded before my eyes surrounded in an eeriness that no Hollywood director could ever recreate. Time froze. Tunnel vision set in. There was no sound other than my breathing. There was no roar from the crowd, not even a low murmur.

I set up behind home plate trying to look and feel as comfortable and 'at home' as any left-handed-pitcher-posing-as-a-catcher could. I held my glove at dead center over the plate. I had it raised to where I guessed knee-high ought to be. The old-timer's first pitch to me (with no warm-ups) hit the palm of my hand in excess of eighty-five miles per hour with only that wafer-thin piece of rawhide to cushion the blow. Except for my glove flying back and hitting me in the nose and upper lip, I didn't have to move an inch to catch it.

Don't you just hate it when that shit happens? You try to act like nothing's wrong, but your eyes turn red and start to leak and your nose and lip feel like they're swelling up to twice their normal size but they're not. Oh, the shame. I made a feeble attempt to mask it.

"Yeeeooooww!" I said so loudly that everybody in the stadium must have heard me. Then I thought to myself, *No problem.* I slid back a foot or so, believing that he had just gotten lucky, and that moving back a foot or so might help me. I was wrong on both counts.

This time I put my glove low on the inside corner (of a right-handed batter) and said, "Bring it on, Pops." The old guy fired seven or eight more fastballs my way that I didn't have to move a muscle to catch. I probably couldn't have moved anyway. Color me terrified. Those wandering eyes of his were now cutting right through me and his velocity increased a notch or two with every pitch. By this time, most of the other eyes at Durham Athletic Park were focused on me and my wino buddy. Well, they we're definitely watching my new acquaintance. To put it ever so delicately and eloquently in baseball jargon, let's just say he was smokin' my jockstrap off. I wanted out, but I had gone too far to turn back.

I didn't know what to think about this old fogy now and he didn't give me much time to speculate. "They might start jumpin' in or out a little bit now, I don't rightly know," he warned me. His next five or six rounds had to have been at least 90mph and they all had some major movement. I almost had a major movement of my own. "*This can't really be happening*," I thought. This guy looks like he just climbed out of a dumpster and his stuff makes my stuff look like stuff that should be put *into* a dumpster. Each pitch cut the corner of the plate like an X-Acto knife in exactly the same place – knee-high and tight. Thanks to his advanced warning and my strong innate desire to stay alive, I made the slight adjustments to catch his exploding bullets.

"*Hahaha*," I laughed to myself. Then, under my breath I said, "*You made me move my glove*." And I was thirty-something at the time.

By then, all the eyes at the DAP were upon us, er, him. I could hear my own teammates taunting me from the dugout:

"Hey, Allen! Let him borrow *your* uniform," yelled second baseman Welton Pearce.

"Sign him up!" came a direct request from fellow pitcher Kirk Pollard.

"Ain't your arm still botherin' you, Allen?" shouted shortstop Roger Woods.

Truth be known, I was thinking along those very same lines. This old man could bring the rock like I've only dreamed and lied about. He was showing me up, and I mean *badly*, but I was enjoying every minute of it. Boy, did I feel stupid. I didn't have to chase down any balls out in left field because I was too busy fending for my life. Missing one of those fastballs was not a viable option. A few minutes before, I was worried about having to run down a few wild pitches and this guy was demonstrating better guidance than a Tomahawk cruise missile.

He hurled about four more smokers my way; rising fastballs that would have jumped over anybody's late and futile swing. Some folks say there's no such thing as a 'rising' fastball, that it's not possible for a thrown baseball to rise. Maybe. Maybe not. But I'll tell you what those pitches did do: With all the backspin on the ball, once it reached the halfway point to the plate, it stayed on the same plane (the same height from the ground) for the rest of the trip. Gravity was nowhere to be found. Hence, the rising fastball.

'*Who* is *this guy?*' I asked myself more than once. My opinion of this man had changed quite drastically in less than ten minutes. I had been wrong in sizing up people before, but never this wrong. I went from being rather repulsed by his appearance to being immensely impressed by his zeal and determination, not to mention awestruck by his pinpoint accuracy with a rock-hard, sun-dried baseball.

Boxcar Willy looked a little winded by then and said that he'd had enough. Well, it may have been me who said it, but who cares about such trivial matters? Anyway, we left the bullpen by mutual agreement and headed for the gate. As we walked back toward the dugout, I asked him his name two or three times, but he avoided the question each time by saying, "I was up there in the high nineties today, had to be. Just had to be!"

I was thinking he could very well be correct, but I didn't think so. I knew he was damn close and in the 90-mph neighborhood with those last five or six pitches. Although I was still in a state of semi-shock from what I had just experienced, I had a game to pitch in two minutes and I wasn't anywhere near ready to play ball.

"See ya later," I said as we reached the gate, but when I extended my right hand to shake his, the smiling face he'd been wearing since we'd started throwing turned very serious.

"No. Better not," he said, as he took off his glove and offered me his left hand. I didn't have time to question this peculiarity for my team had taken the field and was ready to do battle. I did, however, take note of how weird it feels to shake left hands. Try it sometime with someone and you'll see what I mean.

With no time to stretch, jog, or even run a few sprints, I climbed the mound with that little gremlin named Trepidation crawling all over my ass. I saw the old guy in the stands behind home plate as I tossed about ten warm-up pitches before the first batter stepped up. He was still there three batters later when I pulled up lame running to back up a throw to the plate. I semi-silently cussed myself *and* that old geezer because I hadn't had the time to stretch and get physically prepared to play. *Thanks a lot, Geezer!* Phil Johnson came in to pitch, got us out of trouble, and finished the game on the mound.

After the pain subsided in my torn right calf, I limped through the bleachers a couple of times during the game (which we won, by the way, 7-3, no thanks to me) trying to find the old fellow. I was very curious about his background and where he came from, besides out of left field, I mean. On my way back to the dugout after my second search for the man, I got to thinking maybe the whole thing didn't even happen. This old man and his extraordinary fastball couldn't be for real. I didn't see Alan Funt and the Candid Camera crew hiding in the corners, so it couldn't have even been fake-real. It didn't happen. I got hit in the head with an errant throw during warm-ups and dreamt the whole thing while floating through Coma County.

When I got back to the dugout and propped my leg up on the water cooler, I decided to forget about this strange episode. *It didn't happen, it didn't happen, it didn't happen,* I repeated in my mind.

Stacy strolled over to get a cup of water and said, "Where's your flame throwin' octogenarian, White?" showing off his extensive vocabulary. "You shoulda put him in when you, uh, hurt yourself. Got any sunflower seeds?"

I guess it did happen.

Stacy wandered off searching for seeds and, after a few minutes, I wandered back out to the bleachers in search of the old timer. I knew the guy couldn't have been in his eighties, no way, but I really didn't know what I knew at the time. The crowd consisted mostly of the players from both teams' wives and kids, but there were some other local folks there I'd never seen before, including some kids who had asked us to autograph some baseballs for them when we first arrived at the stadium. I was determined now to find him. I wanted to discover more about him and his baseball past, but he was gone.

Pirates with the Bull Durham Mini World Series trophy: Back row (l-r) Todd Pearce, Stacey Overman, Roger Woods, Randy Pearce, Walt Perry, Kirk Pollard, Don Ussery. Front row (l-r) Allen White, Phil Johnson, Jim Young, Welton Pearce, Mac McDaniel, Ricky Strickland. The little boy in between the front and back rows is Randy's son, Brandon. The bullpen is in the background.

Chapter 2

Dᴜʀɪɴɢ ᴛʜᴇ ɴᴇxᴛ ꜰᴇᴡ ᴡᴇᴇᴋꜱ, this incident replayed itself in my mind at least a thousand times. Okay, perhaps that's overkill and 500 would be closer to the truth, but it happened a lot. I'm not going to say that I was obsessed by what happened that Sunday afternoon, but in retrospect, I can't definitively say that I *wasn't* obsessed either. The jury is still out.

Driving the car or truck became somewhat dangerous for me. While cruising down the highway, I allowed myself at times to drift through the myriad images of that magic, mystical day when something – the loud POP of the old man's heater resounding in my glove – would snap me back to my senses. Instantly, I'd come out of the trance, realize I'd been physically operating a motorized vehicle with my mind on autopilot, and not have a clue as to where I was, where I'd been, or where the hell I was going. Scary. It wasn't just while driving, either. I burned a few steaks, chops, and chickens on the grill, too, and one time I forgot to add sugar to the Kool-Aid lemonade. Nasty.

I made a point of telling everyone who'd stand still long enough my little story about the old man and what had happened. I shared it with my coworkers, customers at work whom I knew personally, our preacher, and even my wife, Pam. When it came to baseball, Pam didn't know her bunt from first base, but she thought it was "interesting" as in, "That's interesting and so are these antique chairs I found at a yard sale that you need to sand and varnish for me."

Okey dokey, then.

My son Jameson had just turned seven and being a big fan of the movie *Field of Dreams*, he wanted the old timer to be Shoeless Joe Jackson "come back to life for real," he said. Most of the folks I told the story to thoroughly enjoyed it, though a few doubters had the gall to give me that tilted-head, puzzled-dog look, like I had three eyes or something.

The more I thought about it, the more convinced I became that this old man was a fine pitcher at some time for some team somewhere. Hell, he was *still* a fine pitcher! Nobody throws that kind of heat with that kind of control only once in a lifetime. This was no fluke. He had done it before; I was sure of it, but when? Where? Was he a former big leaguer who's just a little down on his luck? Bad investments? No investments? Alcohol? Drugs? All the above? Perhaps he was older than I had first estimated, even older than Stacy had joked about. Maybe he had pitched against Walter Johnson or Dizzy Dean! Whoa. Maybe he *was* Walter Johnson or Dizzy Dean!

The imagination can be a dangerous thing sometimes.

I knew Walter and Dizzy were both long dead, so I flushed that idea away immediately, but it left skid marks. Probably just some cinematic residue left behind from watching one particular baseball movie a few times too many. *Field of Dreams* is undoubtedly one of the great baseball films of all time, but the fact remains that it is not a true story. It's a great work of fiction, but I think all people who love the game of baseball want to believe in its limitless possibilities, if nothing else. Ghosts in the cornfield? Gimme a break. And pass the butter. And the saltshaker.

One day in early November, I was in a sporting goods store when I noticed a plastic bucket on the counter beside the cash register. It was full of clear-wrapped packages of black and white remakes of 1910-1950 baseball cards (the Conlon Collection). Each pack contained twenty cards with only the one in the front and the one in the back visible (duh!). I began browsing innocently, trying to see if I recognized any of the names or faces. When I got to the last of the thirty or so packages, there was my hero, Dizzy Dean. I turned the darn pack over, and there, on the other side was, you guessed it, Walter Johnson.

DIZZY DEAN
ST. LOUIS CARDINALS – PITCHER   1934

I nonchalantly tried to talk myself out of thinking that the old-timer I had met that day in Durham might be featured on a card sandwiched somewhere there between those two aforementioned greats. I was doing a decent job of it, too, and I almost made it to the door when it happened. I heard that voice again.

"*Buy it and be sure,*" it whispered. I thought, "*Oh, no. Not this shit again.*" At first I thought it might be the store manager trying to make a subliminal sale. But no, he was back in the storage room reshelving the four pairs of spikes I had tried on but couldn't afford to buy. I may have led him to believe they didn't fit properly, but that's not important. I didn't want to make a fool of myself by haggling with someone or something that may or may not have been there, so I left a buck twenty-five on the counter for the $1 pack of cards and hit the street.

Safe in my truck, but visibly shaken by the way I bumped my head getting in, I peeled the cellophane away from the cards. I scrutinized Dizzy and Walter very carefully and determined that even with some serious and/or celestial plastic surgery, neither could have been the man I was looking for. Of the eighteen remaining cards, only six were pitchers. I separated these from others and began scouring the half dozen faces with a Cracker Jack magnifying glass I kept in my glove compartment. Numbers one through five slowly bit the dust. I was down to my last card.

My last card was turned to the backside which included the player's name, his hometown, and his career stats. Nothing really rang a bell until I read that this particular player hailed from Wilson, North Carolina, a scant twenty-four miles from good old Zebulon. BING! Not quite BINGO, just yet.

In the rearview mirror, I saw a thin sheen of sweat forming on my forehead.

What's that noise?

Is that a drum roll?

I turned the card over and took a good look at the mug in question. When I saw the face, my heart fell through the seat, hit the floorboard, bounced back up through the seat and wound up stuck sideways in my throat. The hooded eyes, the broad nose, the innocent smile, and the wiry build – all wrong! It can't be this clown; he ain't even close.

Man was I pissed.

Chapter 3

THE STORY SHOULD HAVE ENDED HERE. In fact, I did end it there. What I didn't know was this was just the first of quite a few premature endings for this story. Yogi never knew just how right he was when he said, "It ain't over 'til it's over." And then sometimes, it *still* ain't over.

At the time, our baseball league had more than twenty-five thousand players nationwide and a great magazine, HardBall, which was published quarterly. I thought the guys would enjoy reading about this true, but extremely weird occurrence, so I decided to write it all down and send it in just to get it off my chest, once and for all, and to get our Central North Carolina league some ink. The old man's disappearing act after I was injured gave me the perfect angle and everything else fell neatly into place. Even though I chose to steal part of the title, *Phantom of the Bullpen* is a true story. All I had to do was remember it.

I mailed the 6-page story to HardBall's editor in California sometime in late November and by Christmas, I had forgotten all about it.

NOT!

I tried to forget. I tried not to think about it. I tried not to be too let down when I checked the mailbox every day and found nothing from the magazine. Fact is, I was actually hurt by the absence of a response. I thought the story was plenty good enough for HardBall. If I had claimed the guy was Elvis reincarnated and I was pregnant with his love child, we could have made the front page of the National Enquirer, but I didn't want to see it published *that* badly.

Still no word by mid-February and then out of the cold blue, Hardball editor David Krival called me at work. He said that he loved the story, but he didn't know whether or not to believe it. I told him there were close to forty players and about fifty or sixty fans who saw the same thing I did and I was confident that I could get some of them to back me up. He told me that wouldn't be necessary, but there were a few small changes he would like for me to make before he could put the story in a future issue of <u>HardBall</u>.

Mr. Krival then mentioned off-handedly that after the story appeared in <u>HardBall</u>, he felt sure that we could sell it to one of the large monthly sports magazines and make "a couple thousand bucks." Remember that major movement I almost had back in October? I almost had it again.

"That sounds great," I said, trying to contain myself. "What are the changes you want me to make?" I asked, still struggling not to have an untimely and embarrassing out-of-body experience.

"I don't really care for the ending," Mr. Krival stated stiffly. He added, "The bit about the sporting goods store and the old baseball cards, all that crap has to go."

"No problem, sir," I beamed, smiling inwardly to myself at his unintended pun. "Is that all?" I asked, spotting a very easy way out. Wadding up the last two pages of a 6-page story couldn't be all that difficult.

He was supposed to say "yes" and I was all ready to say "thank you" and "good-bye" but that's not how it went down. Remember? I don't have that kind of luck.

"No, here's the thing," the editor said matter-of-factly. "I want you to find this old guy, interview him, get a few pictures, and end the story with his story." Before I could even formulate my mild but legitimate complaint, he said, "You have until April 30th." Click.

"Uh, hello?"

Imagine my joy and confusion. A story I wrote is going to be in a national magazine and all I have to do is locate a certain wino or ghost in the big city of Durham, North Carolina. Yes, my head was shaking again, and I think I even rolled my eyes at myself, which is kind of strange now that I think about it.

Since I had to come to grips with reality, I admitted to myself that this old man could not have possibly been a ghost. When I was a little boy and inquired about ghosts, my grandma set me straight. "When people die, they go to Heaven or they go to hell," she said confidently, thumping first her bible, then my head. "The ones who go to Heaven don't want to come back; the ones who go to hell can't get back. Any questions?"

"No, ma'am." And that was that.

Now I was stuck with my ex-pro-down-on-his-luck theory. Finding a wino in Durham would be easy: go downtown, cover my eyes, throw a rock, and I'll hit one. But finding one particular wino in Durham was going to be the trick of the century, and I ain't no David Copperhead.

There was a lot to think about here. Sadly, if not obviously, thinking is not really my strong suit. All my life I've always tried to avoid such nonsense at any cost. That's one of the reasons I married an accountant with two degrees. Just kidding. Still, there were questions I had to answer on my own and I didn't like it one darn bit. Am I doing this for the money? A few grand for what? Simply recording something that happened right in front of me? Hardly seems fair.

Sure, who wouldn't love to call himself a writer and make a little extra folding money sitting on his ass banging out words on a typewriter, but is that what I'm really after? I do love to write; there's no denying that. Every now and then I run into Joanne Chilton, ex-wife of my best friend from high school, and she always reminds me about a story I wrote on her behalf for a history assignment.

I never did my own homework, shunned it like the plague that it is, but I had no trouble helping someone else with theirs. Hers was a short piece about Roman culture, and I had included a sunny afternoon 'game' at the Coliseum where the Christians were slaughtered by the Lions, 74-0, in the top of the first inning. She got an A and I got a friend for life.

But this baseball story about a man with a set of skills that defy all logic and reasoning, and even if I tell it correctly, is not going to make me a writer. The story is writing itself; I'm just the keyboard guy. When I realized this basic truth, I concluded to just ride it out and see where it leads. No matter what happens, I can always just give up, quit, and walk away, right?

Right.

Chapter 4

I MUST HAVE USED UP ALL THE LUCK allotted to my whole life in one shot when I made the first telephone call to begin my quest to track down the phantom of the bullpen. 'The Voice' didn't tell me to, even though it would have fit in perfectly right about here, but the morning after I talked with Mr. Krival, I called Bill Smith, the manager of the Twins. I asked him if he had ever seen the man before or if he knew anything at all about him.

"Sure, he came to watch one of our practices last spring," Bill said. "He threw balls into the fence for about an hour. None of my guys have the balls to catch him!" I waited. "Son of a bitch throws the ball hard, doesn't he?"

I said, "Bill, I caught him for about ten minutes that day before our game back in October and my damn right hand is still sore." I made a fist with my right hand and, no shit, it was still a little tender. "Can you tell me something about him that I don't know? Maybe his name or which bridge he lives under? Anything! I'm kind of desperate here."

Bill paused for a second then said, "Well, I think Erskine told me that the old fellow lives out in the countryside near him and comes to their practices occasionally."

Suddenly I realized he was referring to Wayne Erskine, a former Dodger minor leaguer, our current Central North Carolina league president, and manager of the Wake Forest Dodgers.

I'm not real sure if I said 'thanks' or 'good-bye' to Bill Smith because the next thing I knew I was talking to Mr. Erskine on the phone. Ten minutes later I had the first name and a telephone number for a man I thought was a nameless, homeless wino, plus Erskine's personal summary of the guy. The Wake Forest skipper politely conveyed to me that he thought the old guy was 'Strange' with a capital S.

"Well, Wayne," I prodded as facetiously as I could, "what's so strange about an old man with a 90-mile an hour fastball?"

"That's not it, Allen," Wayne said. "He thinks we're a farm team for the *Los Angeles* Dodgers."

"So?"

"He wants to pitch for us so he can get a tryout with the real Los Angeles Dodgers."

"So?"

"We're just scared he might get hurt, Allen, and it's not only that. We let him pitch batting practice one day, and after every third or fourth pitch he threw, he walked around to the back of the mound and slammed his glove down in the dirt."

"So?"

Wayne was getting pretty fed up with me saying "So?" and he told me so in some words I can't seem to find anywhere here on my keyboard. Son of a *what*? Kiss your *what*? What I couldn't figure out was why the Dodgers, a team that gets beat *to death* regularly because they have no pitching, wouldn't give a man a chance to pitch who unquestionably throws better than any pitcher in our league.

With his patience worn down to just a few molecules, Wayne finally said, "You have the man's number, Allen, call him yourself and see what YOU think!" Dial tone.

Uh, hello?

At this particular juncture, I have to admit there are some verifiable rumors I may have done some things in my youth that the medical experts say could cause me (and some other children of the 1960s and 1970s) to experience a few debilitating flashbacks from time to time and maybe even have some recurring hallucinations. There's also some stuff about chromosomal damage and birth defects, but just thinking about all that scares me to death.

In order to pursue this story properly, I was now forced to ask myself some very tough questions: Did I, in fact, see that old man do what I saw him do? Since I didn't have a lot of experience in the thinking department, my quick answer had to be yes, but even *I* couldn't take my own word for it. Was the whole thing a flashback of some sort, and if so, a flashback from what? Was I hallucinating? If it was indeed a hallucination, it was a mass hallucination because I wasn't the only one who saw it. Either way, to move forward, I was going to have to find out for sure.

Thoughtfully and thoroughly I jotted down about twenty questions to ask the old guy. I had it all figured out. I'll call him this afternoon and do the interview, drive to his house the next morning to take a quick picture, finish the story that evening, and let the U.S. Postal Service do the rest.

With any luck at all, that would have been it – jack, ching, botta bing; three up, three down, ballgame! But this is me we're talking about here and luck and Allen don't frequent the same circles.

I could never even cheat and get any luck. The only rabbit's foot I ever had did some serious damage to our new washing machine. My grandmother was REAL happy about that. The nail that held up the horseshoe above my bedroom door proved to be not quite long enough on three different occasions: top of the head, right shoulder, and the pinky toe on my left foot as I stomped through the doorway, pissed off about something stupid, no doubt. A few years ago, I was laid up with a bad back for a few days after bending over to pick up a shiny new penny.

Hey, it was heads up. I didn't have a choice!

That one cent cost me about $85 for a doctor visit and a prescription. I think someone who knows me well must have coined the phrase, 'If it wasn't for bad luck, he'd have no luck at all.'

Jack, ching, botta bing, my ass.

Chapter 5

AT AROUND 3:30 THAT AFTERNOON, I dialed the number Wayne Erskine had given me and on the fourth ring, the call was answered by a very sweet but hesitant female voice. "…Hello?"

"Hi!" I said, with some chirp in my voice. "Could I speak with Max, please?"

A few seconds of delay; just enough to make me uncomfortable.

"Max doesn't live here," the sweet voice told me. "I'm his sister, Mrs. Doris Davis. I can get a message to him *if* I deem it necessary." Gone was the hesitation and in its place was something like an authoritative protective shield. I was impressed. And back on my heels even though I was sitting down. Mrs. Davis then asked, "Who are you and why do you want to speak with Max?"

I identified myself to Mrs. Davis as best I could. I told her my story, then I told her about the story I had written, and then I told her about having to change my story.

Even through Ma Bell's quiet static, I could tell that she was not the least bit impressed by any of my stories. At least three times I had to answer the five big 'W's: Who? What? When? Where? Why? Finally, she began to show me a little trust when it was hit upon that we both attended Baptist churches.

Praise the Lord!

After telling Mrs. Davis yet again about meeting Max at the game that Sunday in October, she told me, "You should have been in church instead of on a ballfield somewhere." She sounded so much like my fire and brimstone freewill Baptist grandmother, I had to tell her.

"You sound just like my fire and brimstone freewill Baptist grandmother," I said, immediately wishing I hadn't. I meant for it to be a compliment, but it came out more like an accusation. Quickly I added, "But just for the record, ma'am, I did go to church that morning. The game was in the afternoon."

From there, she told me about her church, Woodland Baptist, and asked me some more questions about my church, Wakefield Central Baptist, and some other stuff before we finally got back to why I had called.

The phantom's name is Gaius "Max" Mangum and he had just turned sixty-two a few weeks before our chance meeting at Durham Athletic Park. I talked with his tough-as-nails but delightfully charming sister for nearly an hour on the telephone that day. And yes, I had to ask her, "Your husband isn't related to 'Crash' Davis by any chance, is he?"

"No, no. I don't think so," she said. "Crash? No. Heavens, no! What kind of a name is that for somebody?"

I know. It's hard to believe, but not everyone saw *Bull Durham*.

Mrs. Davis went on to mention many other things that I definitely made mental note of, but I was just a working stiff, a half-assed salesman, and a weekend baseball player, not a seasoned reporter, researcher, or interviewer. I failed to follow up with pertinent questions to flesh out and clarify many of her statements. In my defense, at the time I didn't fully understand the width, breadth, and depth of what I had stumbled into five months back.

That one big failure would haunt me for a long, long time.

In our way too-brief conversation, I learned some bits and pieces about Max and his sad, but hopeful life. For some unfathomable reason, Mrs. Davis, Max's only protector at the time, seemed to think that I was out to embarrass Max and her family, hence her defensive posture.

She told me that Max had been diagnosed as a paranoid schizophrenic in his late teens and she wasn't too keen on the idea of a story about Max being printed in a magazine or anywhere else. I hadn't even considered the possibility of someone thinking that I would try to hurt Max or his family.

At that time, the only outcome I wanted from this story was fairly straightforward. I wanted baseball players everywhere to know that there was a guy out here in his sixties who was throwing the baseball 90 miles per hour and had the control – not just to throw the ball for strikes consistently – but to put the son of a bitch inside a Dixie cup consistently. That was and still is the whole gist of this story.

Give it a shot sometime and let me know how that turns out for ya.

Sensing that Mrs. Davis already had the wrong idea about me, I backed off with my inquisition. I had never been one to press, hound, or aggravate someone for information or anything else. Pushy, nosey people get under my skin and close to the bone, and I sure didn't want to become one of *them*. So, for almost three decades, there was a gap in this story – right here.

A big gap.

In March of 2021, nearly thirty years after I should have done it, I closed that gap. I finally rounded up enough background information on Max to really make the story complete. On a Saturday morning at Brigs Restaurant in Wake Forest, I had breakfast with and interviewed two of Max's cousins – Curtis Harrison and Sanford Bailey – who were also his closest friends.

I added the things I'd learned on the phone from Mrs. Davis in 1992 with recollections from Mr. Harrison and Mr. Bailey to piece together some of Max's early life. Also weaved throughout the story is information gleaned from an interview with Phil Johnson of Johnson-Lambe Sporting Goods, not to be confused with Phil Johnson who was a pitcher for the Zebulon Pirates.

There are no storybook lives until someone writes the story, and if anyone ever deserved to have their life story told, it's Gaius Max Mangum.

Chapter 6

GAIUS MAX MANGUM was born on Monday, September 16, 1929, about a month before the stock market crashed, igniting the Great Depression. Max's father, Samuel Gaius Mangum, was a hard-working dairy farmer in rural Wake County, North Carolina. The family owned several hundred acres of land a few miles north and west of the then college town of Wake Forest. Big-city bucks beckoned and the Wake Forest College campus moved to Winston-Salem in 1956. The town survived the exodus of the prestigious institute of higher learning and remains a thriving suburb of Raleigh.

Samuel was married to Susie Bailey Mangum and Max was their fourth child. Max had one older brother, Burley, and two older sisters, Doris and Burma. As the baby of the family, Max received the traditional extra attention and thrived as a rambunctious and curious youngster who was always getting into one thing or another: a hornet's nest, tipping over the family cows, or downing a gallon or two of milk that was meant to go to market.

Max also excelled at making himself scarce when it came time to do the daily chores. One good thing Max got into in his youth, though, was baseball. But more specifically, he developed a love for throwing a baseball that stuck with him for the rest of his life.

Max's father died in 1942 from injuries suffered in a fall from one of the large barns that were scattered about the farm. Already a very impressionable youth, the accident deeply affected the 13-year old. Mrs. Davis said she could see some changes in Max even then, but she didn't elaborate. Max's cousin, Sanford Bailey, said, "Max worked a little bit on the farm when his father was alive, but his mother and sisters coddled him after Samuel's death and Max did pretty much what he wanted to do after that." He said Max wasn't doing any of his chores and that gave him plenty of time to do the thing he loved most: play baseball.

As a teenager in the early- to middle 1940's, Max grew up like most of the other boys across America, idolizing the New York Yankees or the St. Louis Cardinals or some other baseball team. They don't call it 'the national pastime' just to pass the time. The first half of the decade was dominated by World War II and names like Adolph Hitler, Joseph Stalin, and Benito Mussolini. The game of baseball was temporarily robbed of many of its players who were off defending their country between early December in 1941 and the middle of 1945. Guys with names like Ted Williams, Hank Greenberg, and Joe DiMaggio.

Max played as much baseball as he possibly could: pickup games, Little League, Pony League, and high school baseball. When he couldn't find a game to get into, he would paint a strike zone target on one of the many wooden sheds on the farm and let the fastballs fly. Curtis Harrison, Max's 1st cousin and best friend, said, "Max totally destroyed three small storage sheds – using nothing but a baseball."

How many people do you know who can annihilate a wooden shed with a baseball?

I know of only two.

Aside from Max, the other guy was a minor league pitcher in the Baltimore Orioles organization who came along in the late 1950's and early 1960's. Steve Dalkowski's name would be as equally recognizable as the names of Walter Johnson, Bob Feller, Bob Gibson, and Nolan Ryan except for one thing: Dalkowski had zero control. We're talking none here, folks. Nada. Zilch. Nil.

To simply say that he was wild would have been a grave understatement. 'Grave' as in the 6-foot deep variety. Dalkowski was downright dangerous. In the movie *Major Leagues*, Charlie Sheen's character Ricky "Wild Thing" Vaughn, is loosely based on Dalkowski's lifelong trouble locating home plate.

I'm simply going to add a sobering thought here: Max would have been thirty years old in the summer of 1960. That's primetime for a baseball player, especially a pitcher. He had Dalkowski's velocity on his fastball and his own exquisite command of placing the ball exactly where he wanted it to go. But he also had a thing called paranoid schizophrenia. I will always wonder what the history of major league baseball would look like if Max Mangum had not been stricken with that truly game-changing disability.

In his best season in the minor leagues, Dalkowski struck out 261 batters and *walked* 261 batters. It was also said that he, too, could throw the ball through a board. While Dalkowski would have needed a barn-sized board to prove that feat, Max could throw the baseball through the peephole of an oak door if you asked him.

There were no devices to record the speed of pitches back then, but many who had seen Feller pitch said Dalkowski was faster. Like, way faster. Like, probably 10 miles per hour faster, which would put his fastball around 110. Many experts say 110 miles per hour is right at the edge of what is humanly possible. Not many guys want to hit against a guy throwing the ball 100 miles per hour with decent control. Even fewer want to get into the batter's box against a guy throwing it 110 miles per hour with absolutely no control.

Yeah, like, none. I counted 'em.

Mrs. Davis told me, "Max was a promising pitcher in high school. He was looking forward to playing college ball in his hometown, but he was already having problems." Again, she did not elaborate and I was already overwhelmed by all I was learning about Max. When I should have been asking follow-up questions, I was fumbling around trying to get my pen out of my pocket protector. Apparently, I'd never heard of a tape recorder.

In 1947 or 1948, Max enrolled at Wake Forest College after graduating from Wake Forest High School, but in the deep recesses of his mind, something was already amiss that no one knew anything about – not even Max.

At first, there was just a slight change in his demeanor and how he got along with and related to his family, friends, and others. It seemed that Max was putting up walls around himself to keep at bay those who cared about him the most. Getting through those walls required a ton of patience and sometimes even that didn't work. Within the next five years, those invisible walls came tumbling down and some solid walls took their place.

"Max really lost it one day," said Mr. Harrison. "I think it was maybe 1954 or 1955, but don't quote me on that."

Uh, sorry. Too late now, sir.

"It was a Sunday morning and Max went over to his brother Burley's house and just started tearing it apart," he continued. "I know it was a Sunday because we'd all got dressed up to go to Sunday School but we never made it to the church." Mr. Harrison then said, "The sheriff arrived around noon and took Max away. The family was in shock. It was a long time before many of us saw him again."

After that episode, according to Mr. Harrison, Max was never quite the same.

The last thing Mrs. Davis told me that day on the phone in February of 1992 was that "all mental illness was treated with shock therapy back then" and Max was zapped regularly for the next twenty years. From what I gathered from her accounts, Max had absorbed and accumulated enough voltage to graduate from nervous exhaustion and depression to earn an AC/DC degree in paranoid schizophrenia.

Well, that little bit of information really got me thinking, which is never a good thing, considering the source of those thoughts. Dorothea Dix Psychiatric Hospital in Raleigh became Max's home away from home. He was in and out of their doors from 1950 through 1975, possibly longer. I can't even begin to imagine what that must have been like. Max didn't have a clue as to what may have been wrong with him. The doctors had an idea of what may have been wrong with him, but virtually no clue as to what to do about it.

In my imagination, I can see Dr. Kilowatt discussing Max's diagnosis with Dr. Ampere. Looking over Max's chart, Dr. Kilowatt says, "Well, it says here that he's hearing things and seeing things that aren't there. I say we hook some of these new electrode thingies to his head, since that's where the confusion seems to emanate, throw the switch, and see if that helps. What do you think, Dr. Amp?"

An almost imperceptible nod from Dr. Ampere.

All the lights in Raleigh and across Wake County dim and flicker when they throw the switch. Then, when I see images not of Dr. Kilowatt or Dr. Ampere, but Dr. Frankenstein rubbing his hands together and smiling, I realize that my imagination has jumped track, demolished the station, and is currently running amok.

Reality check, please! I'm outta here.

Several times during my conversation with Mrs. Davis that day in 1992, I started to give up on the whole idea and just forget about it. The story had become very complicated and I was fairly certain that I wasn't qualified to go anywhere near a word like complicated. I suddenly realized that all of this was way over my head and there's no story here, not one that needs to appear in HardBall anyway.

Mrs. Davis said Max didn't have and definitely didn't need a telephone at his house. "When he had a phone, he would call people at odd hours and there was only one thing he ever wanted to talk about," she said.

Let me guess. Tennis?

"His house isn't far from here." she said, "and I'll arrange any contact or communication with my baby brother."

She told me that Max would let her in his house only once or twice a year to clean it up, and he never cleaned it because he was always too busy practicing his pitching. She said that he didn't bathe regularly either, and he used the same excuse for that, also.

I thought to myself, *Hey! What's wrong with that? My son and I use that excuse all the time to get out of a late-night bath!* Then she mentioned that her husband, Edwin, was out at Max's place "at this very minute trimming the weeds around his little practice field."

This was the turning point for me.

When she told me that Max practiced there all alone, all day, every day, I knew I had to see him again. I didn't give a damn about the story anymore. Even greed has a limit. I had found a man who had a 'field of dreams' long before Kevin Costner figured out which end of the bat to hold.

How does someone become so obsessed with the game of baseball that it takes up all of their waking hours? I love the game as much as anyone I know, but I don't think I could handle it 24/7/365. How does a man get to this point? How can baseball become such a focal point of a person's existence? I didn't know the answer to any of these questions at the time, but I was determined now more than ever to find out.

At the end of our conversation, I asked Mrs. Davis to arrange a meeting for Max and me the very next day, but due to several things going wrong on my end, I had to postpone that meeting several times. It was a little more than a month later, the first day of April 1992, before I finally got the chance to see Max for the second time.

Chapter 7

"Max Mangum, paranoid schizophrenic, good to see ya," Max introduced himself and smiled as we shook left hands again. I'm telling you, shaking left hands is one weird sensation. If Gomer Pyle had tried it with someone, I know what he would have said, swinging his head with each word:

Awkward, awkward, awkward.

Without all the hoopla and pressure of an impending game bearing down on me this time, I felt much more relaxed. Not really. I was nervous as a cat on the hot tin roof of a burning woodshed filled with fireworks.

Max, if I'm not mistaken, was wearing basically the same attire he had on that day in Durham. His khaki pants were a little overdue for an ironing, but so was his red flannel shirt and his dark blue nylon jacket. I think his socks may have been white at one time, and maybe his sneakers, too, but they weren't that day. I noticed I was wearing about the same stuff as Max, albeit a tad fresher. This fashion observation coming from a guy who wore the same pair of blue jeans and ratty old Lynyrd Skynyrd t-shirt every single day for about six months when he was twenty-two and in the middle of one of his nomadic periods. Don't even ask me about underwear.

Again, I think I caught Max about three days after his last shave.

"Hi, Max. Allen White, yet to be diagnosed correctly, and it's good to see you, too," I said. We both leaned back against my truck and then I asked, "How ya doin'?"

Max considered this question for a few seconds then roared, "I'm doin' all right, but they say I'm crazy!"

"Aw, that's ok, Max," I responded. "Most of the folks I know are crazy, me included, we just haven't been caught yet."

Max gave me the single 'That's about what I figured' nod and then looked away into the distance and sighed. After a second or two he said, "Well, you wanna go down to the field and throw a little bit?"

I thought about it for nearly half a split nanosecond and said, "Let's go." I hadn't driven thirty miles and lied to my boss about a dental appointment just to stand around and shoot the breeze.

We piled into my truck and drove a quarter of a mile further down the road Max lived on until he directed me to pull over next to a 3-strand barbed wire fence blocking a narrow path through the woods. We got out and fetched our stuff from the bed of my gray Chevy S-10. Max walked over to the fence and pushed down on the waist-high top strand of wire with his baseball glove for me to step across. When I got across, I returned the favor.

Is that trust or what? One wrong move and suddenly he's Maxine or I'm Aileen.

"Is this your land, Max?" I inquired due to an acute aversion to buckshot in the backside.

"They say it is, and I got papers. But now, I really don't know for absolute sure," he roared.

I wondered if Max's 'they' and my 'they' could be the same folks. My 'they' have been getting me in trouble since I was a small boy, as in: *'They' were throwing rocks at cars, too; 'They' said I could use my BB gun to shoot the windows out of this old house.* I still felt a little uneasy about it, but once again, I had come too far to turn around.

'They' were urging me on.

I didn't hear 'The Voice' while I was out there, but I was sure that Max was hearing some voices. Every now and then he would mutter something about "ever-lovin' double criminals stealing electricity" and some other stuff I couldn't even make out. I got a little paranoid myself.

**Like I said, you'll have to use your imagination, but this is darn close.
It's just a photo I lifted from the Internet and manipulated into
a cartoon.**

We had walked a few yards through the thick forest when the underbrush abruptly gave way to a vast, deep green pasture lined with towering trees coming alive with the gently whispering spring breeze. Talk about your field of dreams. With just a pinch of imagination, one could see the gentle rolling landscape and the imposing oaks and pines slowly morph into an immaculate playing field surrounded by thousands of fans all dressed in different shades of green practicing the wave in the upper decks.

But we just kept walking; who has time to stop and smell the roses?

After making our way across this mirage, we stepped back into the woods and crossed over a small stream, then walked over an even smaller stream on a wooden footbridge. We then passed an enchanting gazebo and came upon an area of what looked to me like a tree-shrouded bullpen, heavily littered with hundreds of those old, weathered baseballs, and a few ragged softballs.

I tried to get into the interview thing a couple of times. I actually whipped out my legal pad and an illegal pen (stolen from by boss that very morning), but all Max wanted to do was throw the baseball. He wearily eyed my camera and didn't appear to be in the posing mood. Using the strap, I hung the camera on the lowest limb of a budding peach tree.

I put the interview and the photo shoot on hold for a while. What I needed to do was satisfy my curiosity about how well this man could really throw a baseball. The looks some people had given me when I told them about 'The Phantom' had me doubting myself lately. I knew what had happened that day in Durham, but without any of my teammates around, it was hard to substantiate.

Since I really wasn't sure what kind of story might come from this encounter, I was ready to get this show on the road. Can he throw the baseball ninety miles an hour or not? Did he really have better control than Greg Maddox or not? Am I crazy or not? Don't answer that last one yet.

Max carried his glove in a brown paper Food Lion grocery bag that contained several more of his dried-out baseballs. He noticed I had a brand new one in my mitt and chuckled at it. "It's good to see one with some white still on it for a change," he said. Since I'd grown up playing with baseballs made out of rags, socks, or newspaper wrapped up tightly with mostly slick and shiny black electrical tape, but sometimes with a lighter color black tape, I knew the special feeling that a real baseball, white with red stitching and perfectly round, could evoke.

We stood about forty feet apart and tossed a couple and Max yelled, "I been out here throwin' at the tire all mornin' waitin' for you, Mr. Pittsburgh Pirate Scout. I'm ready when you are." He used his glove and pointed to an area near the woods, just off to my left.

I didn't catch the name he threw at me right away because I was scanning the area where he had pointed. Then I saw it. The tire he referred to was an old car tire on a rope hanging from a huge branch in a massive oak tree. The noontime shadow of the tire made a small dark spot on a wooden home plate painted white and nestled beneath it in the neatly trimmed grass. I backed up about twenty feet and squatted down to see what Max was really holding, barely fighting off the urge to think 'déjà vu.'

Wait. Mr. WHO?

Max has a weird windup. It's somewhere between none at all and a stretch, but when he unwinds – look out! His first pitch was letter-high and a tad inside (on a right-handed batter). I didn't say anything about the location of the pitch and I noticed that Max seemed just a little bit embarrassed that I had to extend my arm to catch it.

"Just gittin' his attention," Max murmured.

Chin music, I thought.

That first pitch seemed a little slower than what I remember him being able to do the previous October. I started thinking it must have been my overactive imagination running away with me on that fateful day five months back. *Well,* I said to myself, *I have made a whole lotta fuss over nothing.*

Quite naturally, I was wrong again. His next twenty or thirty pitches were right on target and up there in the mid- to high eighties, and eventually into the low nineties again. He stung my glove wherever I stuck it.

"Good pitch, Max. Damn good pitch," was all I could manage to say. I was simply fascinated. A strange, fleeting thought flashed through my consciousness. It was just a piece of a scene from the story "The Elephant Man" delivered, I believe, by a lady friend, and it summed up my current sentiments exactly. I felt very fortunate to have made the acquaintance of one Gaius Max Mangum, very fortunate indeed.

For the next ten minutes or so, I stayed squatted down in the catcher's pose. Both of my knees screamed bloody curses at me, but it was all just so much background noise. I was hypnotized by the constant POP! POP! POP! of rawhide on rawhide. After I stood up, I took off my glove and there was some more raw hide where my palm used to be.

Damn! This guy is almost sixty-three years old, I told myself, *this can NOT be real.*

But it was real. It was real and I knew at that moment this was a story that someone must tell.

While we were throwing, I informed Max about the story I was trying to write and about the money that I might earn from it. I told him I would gladly share the reward with him if the story sold, but he wanted something else.

"I don't really need your money. I need to play some ball," he stated. "I have money for you if you can get me in a game somewhere so I can prove myself." I almost teared-up before I could get myself into macho mode. I knew there were people out there who would take advantage of a situation like this, and some who probably already had.

"I'll think of something, Max. We'll come up with something good for you soon," I offered, volunteering for my teammates as well.

"Stick your glove up inside the tire over there," Max said, helping me out of an awkward situation. I walked over to the tire hanging from the tree, did as I was told, and stepped back. Max took aim from about sixty feet away and let fly with the heater. The ball knocked my glove out of the tire and the small, noontime shadow of the tire never moved off the plate underneath. Lying in the grass a few yards behind was my glove with the baseball still in it. What could I say? Nothing.

I wish I could embellish the scene and say that smoke was rising from the ball and glove, but that wouldn't be true, though they were hot to the touch when I picked them up. Using the backside of my old glove, I wiped away something wet sliding down my cheek.

What the hell?

Max was sure he was throwing the ball a hundred miles an hour. "I know it's up there around a hundred. Has to be! Just has to be," he lamented. "But I bes' be careful what I say around here," he said, looking around suspiciously. Lowering his voice, he said, "Last time I told somebody I was throwin' in the hundreds again, they took me back to Raleigh and operated on my hand." He paused to look at me, then continued, "I couldn't throw hard for a couple of months after that."

Because I had two youngsters at home who said it a thousand times a day, I was thinking, *"Yeah, right."* Then he walked over to me and showed me the scars. The back of his right hand around his knuckles and the three fingers between his thumb and pinky appeared to be crisscrossed and crosshatched by past surgical procedures. I suddenly realized why he had not taken my proffered hand for the handshake back in October and again today. I surmised he had a very good reason for not being an avid hand shaker.

When I overcame my paralyzing, dumbfounded state, we talked a few more minutes and I finally had to tell Max it was time for me to get back to work. Honestly, I didn't want to leave. If he had said 'Wish you'd stay awhile' or 'Hang around a bit' I'm sure I would have lost my job. I couldn't have called in with another excuse because there wasn't a telephone out there in the bullpen at Shade Stadium.

Before I left, I gave Max one of our uniforms and made him an honorary member of the Zebulon Pirates. I left him a few baseballs with some white still on them, too. His ear-to-ear grin was all the thanks I needed. I grabbed my camera and snapped four or five shots of Max before he realized what was going on. When he saw the camera this time he was unaffected and actually gave me a little smile.

It was a guilty little smile now that I think about it.

No, I didn't find a ghost or a phantom or a fallen star, but I felt that I had found something more, much more. I had found a man who has been training for 'The Show' every winter, spring, summer, and fall – every single day that the weather permitted – for the past forty-five years.

That, my friends, is perseverance.

Not to mention the find of a lifetime!

Our paths had now crossed twice; one by accident and one prearranged, but I still didn't know much at all about Max and even less about paranoid schizophrenia. Hell, I was still in the dark on how radios and televisions work. (Still am.)

There were, however, two things about which I was very sure. The first thing I was certain about was that Max believed he should be pitching in the major leagues and the man *did* possess a set of skills that made that claim impossible to deny. He could throw a baseball in the ninety mile per hour range with laser-like control. Even in professional baseball, the percentage of guys who can throw the ball 90-plus dead on target is not large. Probably less than 50% of all major league hurlers are capable of that feat. I know there are some who can throw the ball 10 mph faster than Max. And there are some who *may* have better control, but I don't have any idea who they are. Max truly believes he should be pitching for the Dodgers, the Pirates, or the

Yankees and sitting batters down on a regular basis and racking up the K's and the wins.

The other thing I'm confident about? I'm sure that I believe him.

I get it, though. I understand about the mental disability. Max himself says that he's crazy, others allude to the same thing. I don't perceive him as crazy, but I can see that he is caught up in his own little world and nothing else matters too much to him. I get it, I really do. I realize that he couldn't possibly put up with the rigors of the real training, the travel, the press, the pressure, etc., of being a professional baseball player. I'm not stupid. Really, I'm not.

But one central fact remains: he can throw the damn baseball like half of the guys who do it for money wished they could. I know he is too old, too out of shape, too medically fragile, and too whatever else to actually play at the ultimate level. None of this cancels out the point, however, and the point is that Max Mangum can chunk the damn rock.

I have always been satisfied with *believing* that I could have played major league baseball. If *this* had happened *for* me and *that* hadn't happened *to* me, I *believed* I would have made an indelible mark on the game. According to some, I was the Can't Miss Kid.

Can't miss, my ass.

Chapter 8

IN MY MIND, I was going to play baseball for the New York Yankees, pitch every fourth game in the rotation, and hold down first base or roam leftfield when I wasn't on the mound. I planned on batting third in the lineup so I'd get as many at-bats as possible, just like in high school. *No DH needed for me, Coach. Maybe for that light-hitting shortstop, but not for me, thank you.* I was going to revolutionize the game of major league baseball.

In high school, I struck out a lot of batters. Not with serious heat and unfathomable control, but with some decent heat, a couple of different curveballs, a slider, and a knuckleball even the umpires couldn't believe (or call correctly). In my final three years of high school baseball, I lost two, maybe even three no-hitters and a slew of one- and two-hitters. You have to know baseball to understand how that could possibly happen. One word and it's obvious: errors. College and pro scouts were not looking for guys with losing records. I ended up settling for too many small, inconsequential victories.

I can think of only one hitter that I faced in those three years that I didn't strike out at least one time. His name was Kenneth Bass and he played third base and batted cleanup for Oxford Orphanage High School. Kenneth wasn't tall, but he was built like a 5'8" fire hydrant, which is damn tall, for a fire hydrant.

There was never a problem getting two strikes on Kenneth but getting that third and final strike was like busting rocks with a rubber mallet. It just wasn't going to happen. He'd foul off pitch after pitch after pitch. He'd wear me down and then manage to hit the ball somewhere. We actually ran out of baseballs during one of his at-bats and had to finish the game with balls given to us by the Orphanage team. Embarrassing.

I remember facing a couple of other real tough outs, Guy Currin and Drew Fish, but I know I sat them both down a time or two with the hook. In one of our home games, Guy, from South Granville High School, leaned across home plate and hit a pitch that was a foot outside and a foot off the ground *over* the 60' tall pine trees in dead center field. If I didn't know better, I would have sworn that the ball was still on its way up when it cleared the pines. I had a tough time living that one down. My guys gave me hell for two weeks teasing me about that long tater.

Drew, from Fuquay-Varina High School, was a fierce competitor in baseball and football but was always just a hell of nice guy on the field and off. He'd smile like a possum eating persimmons if I struck him out or if he ripped a screaming laser to the fence in left center. His smile never changed.

I remain friends, not close friends, but friends with both of those fellows.

I led the Capital Area 2A Conference in strikeouts my sophomore, junior, and senior years, averaging 10+ per game and these were 7-inning games. I had 15 strikeouts on several occasions, but the one I'm most proud of was during my junior year against arch-rival Bunn High School, which was only 10 miles away but in a different county. That night, I had 15 K's against a lineup that included seven very good hitters, gave up only 3 hits, knocked in three of our runs, and lost the game 7-4!

Don't ask; shit happens.

I had to strike guys out because I knew that if they somehow managed to put it in play, chances were very good that they would end up on base. My team played like major league all-stars at practice – better than all-stars! Our shortstop, Mark Chamblee, would dive – flat out – to knock down base hits up the middle and throw out fast runners at first base *from his knees.* Second baseman David 'Mushroom' Phillips would pivot swiftly *after eating up a bad hop from a hard grounder* and start a 4-6-3 double play. Our center fielder, William Gay, would storm in hard and fast on a Texas League blooper, make an incredible *shoe-string catch,* and then tumble and roll all the way to the infield. Right fielder Doug Dunn would shade his eyes with his glove on fly balls and then bring it down quickly to make Willie Mays-style basket catches.

If only we could have played games on those practice days.

Come game day, we were the Bad News Bears before there ever was any Bad News Bears. We booted routine ground balls and muffed routine pop ups so routinely, it became, well, routine. I came to expect it after the first few games of my sophomore year and eventually accepted it as just the way it was going to be. I guess I should have been more like a leader and raised hell with my teammates when we screwed up, but you actually need to possess leadership qualities to pull off such a thing, and I just wasn't that kind of player.

The fact that most of the other guys on the team my sophomore year were juniors and seniors had nothing to do with my reticence in dealing with the comedy of errors. No, sir. I didn't like getting my ass kicked by anybody, regardless of what grade he was in. I played my game and expected everyone else to play theirs. Seldom did it work out that way.

Although I had a strong batting average and knocked in a lot of runs, there were two other aspects of my hitting game that I was prouder of after my senior year. First, in three years as a starter in high school baseball, I struck out only five times. Some kid from Franklinton High School got three of those K's in one game my junior year. He had a curve/sinker pitch that simply dropped like a rock off the table straight down right at the back point of home plate. I got in nine good whacks at it but I almost broke my damn neck trying to hit that thing.

My other source of pride at the plate was that I walked even less than I struck out. I don't recall exactly how many bases on balls I received during those three years, but I know there must have been one or two. In my memory bank, though, I have no images of myself ever trotting down to first on a free pass. As I said, there must have been a couple, but I just can't see them.

I always went to the plate with the same plan: if the ball comes anywhere near where I can reach it with this big stick, I'm going to hit it just as damn hard as I can. Yes, there were a few times when I rolled over on a bad pitch and dribbled one to an infielder and wished I'd been a little more selective, but hell, that wastes time! When I got into the batter's box, I was ready right then to put a dent in the ball and get myself in position to score.

With all these accomplishments under my belt, there was no doubt in my mind that I could have played in the major leagues.

Now look who's delusional.

Chapter 9

Wʜᴇɴ ɪ ʀᴇᴀᴄʜᴇᴅ ʜᴏᴍᴇ after work that evening, and the visit with Max earlier in the day still fresh in my memory, the wheels were already turning in my head to plan some kind of tournament so Max could play some baseball. And somehow, I needed to talk my teammates into letting Max pitch for us in one of our games. Within one week and with super support from Jean-Marc Savory and Greg Johnson at the Zebulon Parks and Recreation Department, we organized a baseball tournament for Father's Day weekend in June. There are a lot of small parts that have to work together to pull off such an event, but with the help of God and two friends, we made short work of it.

Since we were hosting this thing, the Zebulon Pirates were definitely going to be one of the four teams representing Central North Carolina of the Men's Senior Baseball League. We held a drawing to determine the three other teams from our league of seven. I contacted Skeeter McCloskie, president of the Research Triangle Area's Roy Hobbs Baseball Association, a rival league, and secured four more teams for the baseball fest.

Each team would play a team from the opposing league one time during the Friday through Sunday event, with double-headers for each team on Saturday. There would be no championship or pressure-filled games, just play good baseball and have fun. Admission to each game for fans, players, wives, kids, umpires, and dignitaries was set at one dollar or one nonperishable food item per game. All the proceeds would go to the Food Bank of North Carolina.

(Side note: In September, three months after the tournament, I received a call from a representative of the NC Food Bank. She just wanted to let me know that some of the funds and food items we'd raised at the tournament were on the way to Homestead, Florida to aid victims of Hurricane Andrew.)

I, too, love it when a plan comes together.

I tend to think that this was one of the best ideas I ever had, but I can't really take credit for it because everything is God-given.

I personally was breaking all kinds of rules by allowing a non-roster player to participate in the games. If Max got hurt or if he hurt someone else with that nuclear powered fastball of his, my ass was going to be in a serious sling. Because my ass already had thirty-six years' experience at being caught up in one kind of sling or another, I didn't give it much thought. Actually, *no thought* would be closer to the truth. Come hell or high water, Max was going to pitch in a baseball game Father's Day weekend.

Considering that my Pirates had four games to play over the course of those three days and only three reliable pitchers at the time, I had to talk my guys into adding Max to our roster, at least for the weekend of the tournament. I had no idea how the guys would react to such a request, and there was only one find out. After doing a little research, I decided to just throw it against the wall and see if it would stick.

A couple of minutes before one of our biweekly practices at East Wake High School's baseball field, I got the guys together in the dugout and told them what was happening. They were all excited about the tournament and everybody was fairly certain they could be there, but there was one more item we had to discuss a little more thoroughly.

"You talkin' 'bout that old man that burnt you a new asshole last fall in Durham?" asked Welton Pearce, coming over to where I was standing to get his customary 'five' on everything he said. He usually got 'five' from everybody anytime anybody said anything on the baseball field. That's just the way he was. He had all of us doing it, sometimes a little bit more than what seemed comfortable. All athletes do it to a certain extent, but it probably looked kind of strange to outsiders as much skin as we exchanged. Welton was definitely the King of Skin.

"He'd be the one," I said, giving my second sacker a 'five' back.

A couple of the other guys looked apprehensively at each other, trying to decide which one was going to broach the subject. A few moments of awkward dead silence passed slowly. The shoe was going to drop; I just didn't know when.

"Ain't he 'bout half crazy?" asked our fleet-footed centerfielder Ricky Strickland, as diplomatically as possible, of course. "I mean, I know he can throw the ball and all, but ain't he off in the head a little bit?"

I thought for a second, made eye contact with most of the guys, and said, quoting what I'd read in a magazine article a few days before, "Howard Hughes, one of the richest and brightest men in the world, sorted the peas on his dinner plate according to size with a specialized pea-counting fork." I looked around; everyone was still listening, so I continued, "During a 2-day period, Hughes watched Ice Station Zebra 150 times in a row on a continuous loop." I was now getting the looks I had anticipated. I added, "His curled-up fingernails and toenails were about a foot in length when he died," I paused for effect and then said, "of malnutrition."

Ricky said, "Now that's just crazy."

"Well, Max doesn't do any of that shit," I said, "but he does have that damn red hot fastball,"

"Sign him up!" Kirk Pollard said, repeating his request from six months ago. Everyone more or less agreed and it was on.

I love these guys.

Welton was already going around giving and getting 'five' from everybody. When he got to me, he gave me 'ten' and said, "This ought to be fun."

Other things were not working out as planned, though. Oddly enough, the pictures I had taken that day while visiting Max turned out to be duds. Technological wizard that I am, I failed to notice that the film in the camera had already been used up in October at a birthday party for my three-year old daughter, Taylor, and at Christmas the previous year. Ansel Adams I ain't, apparently. Lots of cake-smeared smiles, party hats, colorful balloons, candles, wrapping paper, our Christmas tree, Taylor playing with an American Girl doll, and Jameson strutting around with a Ghostbuster backpack, but no Max.

After planning the tournament, I continued to work on my little story about "Phantom of the Bullpen" without actually telling the real story. In the version of the story that I finally submitted to HardBall, I suggested that Max wasn't exactly the guy next door by mentioning in an off-hand way that he was *extremely eccentric*. I made no mention of his mental illness in that version of the story because I felt uncomfortable (and still do, to a certain degree) revealing and discussing someone else's disability for all to see.

I wanted everyone to know about his daily monumental struggle to get over a mountain that can't really be climbed, yet I felt I still needed to protect his privacy. Max is wired to pitch a baseball and not much else. He can't drive and doesn't take very good care of himself. These things, however, didn't belong in *that* story.

His thing, his *only* thing, is to find somebody to catch the heat emanating from baseballs delivered by his right arm. If he can't do that, his thing then is to find somebody to take him somewhere so he can find someone willing to catch him.

And if *that* doesn't work out, he's off to his own little field for an imaginary game. There at Shade Stadium, he throws eighty-one strikes through the tire hanging from the oak tree and fans twenty-seven imaginary hitters. After an imaginary post-game interview, Max takes a long, hot imaginary shower and a little later hits an imaginary bar with a few of his imaginary teammates. While he's there, he has an imaginary beer or three, and then maybe later on he even gets to first base with the prettiest imaginary woman in the joint.

Everything else, and I mean everything: eating, sleeping, cleaning up his house, and coming in out of the rain and cold, is just secondary.

HardBall's slightly edited version of my original 4-page story (sans the last two pages about the sporting goods store and the baseball cards) was published nearly two years later in the spring of 1994. It included no background information about Max because I didn't have very much at that time. The prologue at the beginning of this story wasn't added until ten years later because it took me that long to put two and two together and realize the connection.

I know; I'm slow.

What <u>HardBall</u> published in 1994 was basically a severely abbreviated version of the second half of Chapter 1 and an equally abbreviated version of Chapter 7. The magazine version concluded with the last exchange of words between Max and me that brisk April Fool's Day afternoon at Max's Shade Stadium:

> *...we'd said our good-byes and I was groping for my keys when I noticed again how nice and green everything looked after several weeks of rain and chilly temperatures. "I'm glad to see we're finally getting some good baseball weather for a change," I remarked as I reached my truck. I had stopped to look back to see if Max had heard me when I saw him hang his head momentarily.*
>
> *He said, "Yeah, me too. I just hate that another spring is about to get by me and I still ain't signed a contract with nobody yet."*

Back on that day back in April of 1992, I knew that Max was dead serious and there was nothing in the world I could do about it. For him, it meant another year of throwing strikes through a tire instead of throwing strikes past major league hitters. One more year of anonymity for a man who could have been a legend. One more year of chasing a dream that's not even there. Max wasn't the only one who left Shade Stadium that day with a heavy heart.

So much for your happy endings.

I did some more revising of my little story over the next few weeks after visiting Max at Shade Stadium. In order to beat that April 30th deadline, somewhere around the 25th, I mailed the 'finished' story to the editor in California, sans the phantom photographs that I *thought* I'd taken but didn't get taken.

I didn't have the luxury of waiting until after the tournament in June to finish the story. A deadline is a deadline. It would have been great to have included some pictures of the game and a summary of the tournament, but that just wasn't going to happen. In late June, about a week after the tournament, I sent Mr. Krival the team picture that had been taken after the game that Max pitched on Father's Day. I thought I was wasting my time, but thankfully that photograph accompanied the story in <u>HardBall</u> in 1994.

In that photo, none of us stood any prouder than Gaius Max Mangum.

Anyway, I needed to put this whole crazy story behind me and get on with the business of my life: my wife, my kids, my job, etc.

Chapter 10

My JOB at this time in my life was a joke. I worked for a company that rented and sold construction equipment back when people were actually building things. It seems there was a big downturn in the construction business in the Raleigh-Durham area during the early 1990s. After the first few days of managing the place, I realized that Dennis Equipment Company was actually going out of business. They were paying me more money than I'd ever made, so I kept this little anomaly to myself.

You don't rock the boat if you can't swim.

My specific job there was to do it all: answer the telephone, assist the walk-in customers, keep the mechanics busy, coordinate deliveries and pick-ups for the drivers, and fill in the blanks on the rental contracts. Trouble was, the phone wasn't ringing, nobody was walking in, the mechanics had all the equipment ready, the drivers didn't have much to deliver or pick up, and therefore, there was nothing to put in the blanks on the rental contracts. As a result, from January to March of 1991, I was able to make hundreds of phone calls to put together the Zebulon Pirates baseball team. I got us into a league, located a sponsor, shopped for uniforms and equipment, scheduled fields for our home games, nailed down a manager, and found some batboys.

It was during this same silence in April of 1992 that I was able to plan the Father's Day tournament and grease all the little pieces that made it fly. I tied up every loose end: umpires, entry fees, advertising, secured two baseball fields for three days, bought trophies, and a lot of other stuff that I can't even remember now. By the first day of May, I was cruising.

It was a short cruise.

"Play at the stadium."

My eyes shot open from a not-too-deep sleep. Please don't be that voice again. *"Say what?"* I said to myself.

Was it *The Voice*, or a dream?

"Play at the stadium."

"Why?" I asked. No answer. Then I answered myself, "So Max and the other guys can play baseball in a real stadium with a nice, grassy infield, sweet box seats for their wives, and state-of-the-art dugouts."

I thought that was all, but it wasn't. I then added, "And so *I* can play in a real stadium with all that stuff, too."

So. Perhaps it was me all this time. Sometimes I'm a little selfish. Sue me.

At first I couldn't remember for sure where I got the idea to try and play some of the tournament games at Five County Stadium. The Voice? Who knows? If I could schedule one game for each of the eight teams (four games) at FCS, I'd be the man! Maybe. Maybe I was subconsciously jealous because the team from Durham got to play regularly at Durham Athletic Park. Plausible, but now that I think about it, I'm fairly certain it was slugger Stacy Overman who said something at practice one day like, "Hey, White! Why don't we play some of the tournament games at Five County?"

Yes, now that I've thought it through, I'm sure that was the origin of the idea. Stacy had said it offhandedly like all we had to do was say we're going to play there and that'd be it. I was sure that a bushel basketful of big-time ass-kissing would have to take place before that could happen, and maybe some money might even have to change hands, too. I don't think I was really moved at first by the idea of playing at Five County Stadium, but I guess the thought just sat there, festering in my brain until my brain did whatever it usually does with thoughts in lieu of actual thinking them through.

Whatever. One little change won't hurt anything. Let's do this!

Ha!

The first thing I did was right. I checked the Mudcats' schedule and made sure they were out of town Father's Day weekend. That took all of about three seconds. The next three weeks, however, I recall in a haze of mostly confusion mixed with a little anger.

Anger's hard to gauge, though, so let's call it a pinch or two of serious frustration.

That first year of existence for Five County Stadium (1991) was a most confusing time for the town of Zebulon, the Carolina Mudcats, team owner Steve Bryant, the Triangle Sports Authority (which was created specifically for Five County Stadium), the Wake County Board of Commissioners, and the Zebulon Parks and Recreation Department. The second year wasn't much better. They all thought they were, in some capacity, in control of the new baseball complex located in what was previously a tobacco field owned by Avon Privette.

I started by explaining everything to Zebulon's town manager, Charles Horne, who said my idea sounded 'interesting' and he'd get back to me the next day. *Now, where have I heard the word 'interesting' used that way before?* I asked myself. It was as if I could see him putting the single quotation marks around it with his forefingers.

Mr. Horne didn't call me the next day, or the day after. You see where this is heading? I still hadn't heard from the town manager three days later, so I called the Mudcats' General Manager, Joe Kremer. Joe's a very nice guy, but he was totally clueless as to what I should do, and I mean that in a good way. He had no suggestions but wished me luck.

Still no toot from Horne a week later, so I went down the Triangle Sports Authority rabbit hole. I talked to at least four people there, and none of them had the authority to tell me anything. In fact, all they told me was a whole bunch of nothing, so I won't bother repeating any of it.

Keep in mind that I'm explaining to all these different people and entities exactly what it is that we want to do: baseball tournament, old-timers, Father's Day weekend, proceeds to the Food Bank, etc.

I called Zebulon's town manager again two weeks after he said he'd call me back. Mr. Horne cleared his throat and said, "I'm sorry, but I don't think you guys are going to be able to do your thing."

The hell you say.

I had a very strong suspicion that he hadn't given my request a second thought since the first day we spoke.

I cleared my throat, twice, and told Mr. Horne, "I'm sorry, too, but just because *you* don't think we'll be able to do our thing, doesn't necessarily mean that we won't be able to do our thing." Click!

I wanted to say 'asshole' but I didn't. It was an arduous decision. I didn't know him well enough to make that serious judgement. When in doubt, leave it out.

I also have an acute aversion to political types and bureaucrats, too, so going to the Wake County Board of Commissioners was definitely not an option for me. People have been known to disappear when tangling with that band of outlaws! All things being equal and I had to choose between buck-shot in the backside or deal with some damn bureaucrat? Just shoot my ass.

My last real shot at this thing was Steve Bryant, owner of the Carolina Mudcats. Being an official, lifelong, card-carrying nobody, I could never gain audience with the man, so I simply faxed him our proposal and also reminded him that each team in the Men's Senior Baseball League carried a one million dollar insurance policy against any kind of accident or damage during any of our games and it covered the spectators as well. I may have come across a little too strong and a bit too sarcastic when I reminded him that insurance on the spectators was something he did NOT have for his Carolina Mudcats games and it says so right there on all the tickets.

Another week passed and it was near the end of May and I had to final-ize the arrangements on where the games were going to be played. Earlier in the month, I had told the seven other managers about possibly getting Five County Stadium for half the tournament. They told their players and every-body was pumped about playing there.

Still no word from Mr. Bryant by the Friday before Memorial Day, so I had the dubious honor of calling all the other managers and all my players and telling them that FCS was a no-go. I told them we would be playing the games at the Zebulon Community Park and Zebulon Middle School (my old high school) and to call me here at work if they had any questions. I quickly phoned the Zebulon Parks & Recreation Department and solidified my deal with them for both fields for the weekend of the tournament. More than just a little disappointed, I leaned back in my chair, propped my big feet up on my little desk, and tried to come to terms with defeat.

That task didn't take long at all.

My boss wandered in a short time later, sat on the rusty beige fold-out chair on the other side of my little desk, propped his bigger feet up there and said, "As of five o'clock this afternoon, we are out of business."

Can you say 'unemployment line' boys and girls? Sure you can. Rolls right off the tongue, doesn't it?

In all my years, I'd never been hit in the head with a sledgehammer, but I can't imagine it would feel much differently than that little bit of bad news did. I mean, damn. If my wife didn't have a great job making twice as much money as I did, I would have probably been insanely pissed off at the prospect of not being able to feed and clothe my family or provide them a place to live.

I couldn't really be mad about it, though. The other employees and I had discussed the inevitability of the business going belly-up many times before, so it wasn't a big surprise. It was just bad timing.

A few days later, I was thanking God for this unexpected downtime. This unpaid vacation afforded me valuable time to spend with my family. It also allowed me the quiet time to reflect on my so-called life...

Chapter 11

I was born in the wee hours of the morning on Wednesday, March 9, 1955, at the Glover Clinic in Madison, West Virginia, the seat of government for Boone County.

In a cop-out effort to make a long, sad story short and not dwell too long on things that make me feel uncomfortable, I'll just try and clear things up and start off by saying that I was adopted at birth by my maternal grandparents, Jesse and Marie (Browning) White. This timely maneuver gave me six brothers (Pete, Bill, Clifford, Jackie, Rex, and Mike) and two sisters (Nadine and Anna Lee) who were, in reality, my uncles and aunts. Obviously, this doesn't include my mother, Betty, because that would make explaining this even more complicated.

Pete, at age nineteen, was killed in a car wreck before I was born. Jackie passed away from pneumonia at age twenty-two, when I was around five or six, after an eleven-year battle with muscular dystrophy. It should be easy to see why I want to hurry and get through this part. I am not a big fan of death and there seemed to be a lot of it in my youth.

Except for Pete, who never had the option, all of these fine people accepted me unconditionally as their little brother and in my heart they will always remain my big brothers and sisters.

If you keep in mind that this took place in West Virginia and take into account the jokes we've all heard about Appalachia, it doesn't seem so strange now, does it?

It's ok. Go ahead and laugh. We tell the same jokes about you guys.

My mother, Betty, and my father, Norwood Bentley, were never married and had no other children together. You could say, among other things (watch it, buster!), that they broke the mold when I was born and I guess that's a good thing. My mother married later on and had three children: Mark, Lisa, and Sarah. My father had three other children also: Norwood Bentley, Jr., Esther, and Elizabeth (Liz). In this little family dynamic, speaking (writing) abstractly, of course, I could be the one they call the Seventh Son. Okay. Maybe not.

At least we weren't dysfunctional.

Now let me add all these wonderful people together and see what shakes loose. That's two half-brothers and four half-sisters (though I don't like that 'half-' term at all) to go along with my six brother/uncles and two sister/aunts. So, in summation, I have fourteen siblings! Hey, it's West Virginia. What can I say?

All I know is that I'm the luckiest guy in the world to have them.

In the early 1960's, I learned how to play baseball in the muddy alleys and on the narrow patches of grass between the small and mostly green painted houses of Y&O Coal Camp, about a mile east of Van, which is twelve miles as the crow flies or thirty minutes as the road goes from Madison.

Late in the summer of 1961, at the tender age of six and a half, I fell in love with the game of baseball. It was the perfect set-up. So many things happened, both big and small, that had an incredible, long-lasting influence on such an impressionable young mind. There are images, memories, smells, sounds, and tastes from this time in my life that have always stayed with me. It is simply amazing that I can have total recall of the New York Yankees starting lineup from the early 1960's, and yet I can't remember how to multiply or divide fractions from one day to the next.

I can clearly see my cousin Steve sitting on his front porch next door with his right leg propped up on the whitewashed banister, bright red blood still seeping through his torn white sock from taking a spike while trying to make a tag at third base. I didn't know what the hell that even meant at the time, but it sounded cool as shit. Steve, nicknamed Runt (everybody had a nickname), and my brother Mike were mainstays on the Van High School baseball team. Mike (Sturgell) was a quality pitcher and showed me a thing or three about how to throw a baseball.

My brother Rex (Bear) played baseball, too, but he excelled in football and after graduating high school in 1962, attended New Mexico Highlands University on a full scholarship. A couple of other nicknames I remember from the ballfield and my brothers' generation are the brothers 'Champ' and 'Burr Head' Dingess, 'Panic' Wright, my cousin 'Monnex' White, brothers 'Jar Head' and 'Duck' Jarrell, 'Jinxy' Davis, and 'Chops' Vint. Not to mention three of the semi-notorious Jones' brothers: Cat, Lefty, and Beaky.

Steve also had *two*, not *one*, but *two* shoe boxes full of baseball cards I wish I could get my hands on today. I clearly remember the bubble gum smell of the powdered sugar-coated card with a smiling Willie Mays, the 'Say Hey Kid' on the front. Not to mention every Yankee that had ever put on the pinstripes.

The hot, musty smell of an old mattress my brothers burned up so they could use the springs to drag their baseball field up in Roach Hollow is kind of hard to forget, especially when I mix in the stench of the sizzling flesh of both my palms. Wow. The memories just keep wafting my way. I was jumping over the hot, glowing mattress springs after the fire went out when my toe caught at the end and I went down on my hands. I didn't stay down long, but I was down there long enough to say some words I didn't even know that I knew.

It wasn't more than ten minutes after the bedspring incident that word got back to my house about my little cussing rampage. You can't say enough about the sheer speed and accuracy of the 1960s clothesline gossip network. That report beat me home and I had made an immediate beeline to the house, well, right after I'd stopped crying. My burns weren't all that bad, but I was seeking some tender loving care and a heaping helping of that cure-all salve that my grandmother kept in the medicine cabinet. I'm just glad she didn't opt for the mercurochrome or Merthiolate.

A little later that evening I was feeling better until I found out what a switch felt like on my bare legs and was then introduced to the wonderful taste of Lifebuoy Soap. I was deeply affected, but not particularly impressed with either. Lesson learned, though. If you're going to cuss, don't get caught.

Leather, under any circumstances, just doesn't taste good at all and old leather tastes very bad. I kept pestering Mike until he finally found me a baseball glove of my very own. Lefty Jones had let me borrow his first base-man's mitt a couple of times, but for some reason, he kept wanting it back.

I think Mike got the glove he gave me from Shoeless Joe Jackson, as in, it was last used in the 1919 World Series. It was *that* old, not to mention butt-ugly. It was so old, there was no other glove around like it. The damn thing had only four fingers! It had a big thumb and three other enlarged fingers, but it was somewhat symmetrical, and that allowed me, a lefty, to use it on my right hand. I sure didn't have to worry about anyone borrowing it.

I learned how to catch with that glove and I used it for five years. The only problem was the leather laces worked themselves loose all the time. They were so old, worn, dry-rotted, and short the only way to tighten them up was to use my teeth on the knots. Yuck is right, but what do you do?

Other early memories include talk of the Yankees, Mickey Mantle, Roger Maris, 61 homeruns, breaking Babe Ruth's single season homerun record, and taking the World Series from the Cincinnati Reds four games to one, even though I really didn't understand the concept of 'World Series' at the time. I just figured it was a big thing.

When I got to be about eight, my friends and I would sneak about half a mile up into Roach Hollow to 'Candlestick Park' and watch the older boys play ball. Candlestick was a field they had sculpted from a relatively flat piece of land between the Roach Hollow Branch and the other mountain. They called it Candlestick Park because if you wanted to play a night game, you had to bring candles, and a lot of them. A few times they even let us get in a game if they were short a player or two. Candlestick Park was *the* main attraction in Y&O Coal Camp.

They didn't call it a coal camp simply for the prestige. No, sir.

After a few more years, the kids around my age from just up the road in Sandfield would come to Candlestick Park in the sweet confines of Roach Holler to play ball. The whole scenario had the aura of the movie "Sandlot" but it was the War on Poverty version. Barefoot boys, ragged shorts, and dirty t-shirts opposed to nice sneakers, blue jeans, and colorful t-shirts. Same game, though. They'd talk junk about what a shitty field we had, and we'd say, "Yeah, yeah. At least we got a damn field," and we'd beat them or they'd beat us and we'd chase their asses out of the holler, throwing rocks at them the whole way.

In retrospect, life was very good back then.

Still looking back, I think the team from Sandfield had the original Ichiro. The guy's last name was Rowe, and he was a little older than the rest of us. It seems he'd caught 'something' and had acquired the nickname 'Itchy' because he had kept his hands in his pants for a couple of weeks chasing who knows what.

Itchy Rowe was a darn good second baseman, as I recall, but he couldn't hit worth a shit. We never had more than one baseball and each team had only one or, if we were lucky, two bats to use, so I really hated that I had to pitch if Itchy had handled the ball while they were in the field. I'm just glad I didn't have to bat after him.

At that time in our little Appalachian Shangri La, organized Little League baseball consisted of four teams (Dodgers, Braves, Cardinals, and Yankees) and covered the ages of eight through twelve. When I turned eight, I joined the Yankees, naturally. In my rookie season, I vividly remember stepping up to the plate with my bat on my shoulder, hearing three pitches whiz by (I sure as hell didn't see them), and walking back to the bench with the bat still on my shoulder about *a thousand times!*

In today's world, the age groups are split up a little better to make it more competitive, but I honestly believe that learning to catch up with an older and bigger boy's fastball during the first three of those four years made me a good hitter and helped me develop and refine my hand-eye coordination.

Also in that first year, I started in right field the first two games. I didn't really notice that my name wasn't called out in the starting lineup before we played our third game. When our manager, Dual Loftis, said hit the field, I hit the field. When I got out to my spot in right, there was another damn kid out there! I looked to the bench with the most incredulous look an eight year-old could muster and made an elaborate gesture with my left hand at this pretender, this interloper, but then I heard them calling *my* name to come back in. I cried all the way off the field.

Apparently, there *is* crying in baseball.

I made the all-star team when I was twelve. Yea! Standing around talking to a couple of other guys in center field during all-star batting practice, I heard the sharp crack of the bat, but paid it no attention. I was trying to be cool, waving my arms wildly, demonstrating some stupid thing or another, and the line drive hit right in the webbing of my glove, nearly ripping it off my hand. Needless to say, that scared me badly and I've always paid strict attention while on the field since then. That's the moment I learned to appreciate the unmistakable *thwack* of bat solidly meeting ball.

Well, except for two other times.

I remember standing on the creek bank many summer evenings until it was almost too dark to see, tossing up rocks and bashing them with some kind of stick or a discarded implement handle, high into the mountain. I had never owned a real baseball bat, but I could always find a stick. Sometimes, with a slight breeze in the trees and the river gurgling its way around the bases of two mountains coming together, a hickory stick and a rock can sound a whole lot like ash wood on rawhide.

I vowed not to go home until I hit a rock so far up the mountainside that I couldn't hear it rip through the leaves or bounce off a tree trunk. I think I remember accomplishing that goal a couple of times, but then again, sometimes we all take the liberty of making the past look more like we want it to be rather than what it actually was.

Chapter 12

MEANWHILE, about 225 miles directly southeast of where I was standing at the mouth of Roach Holler in West Virginia in 1966, Max Mangum was probably trying to get into a baseball game somewhere in Raleigh, North Carolina. He had his choice of at least three nice venues: Devereux Meadow, Doak Field, or more than likely, Red Diamond in Pullen Park.

"Max would get me to take him to the Red Diamond field in Pullen Park about two or three times a week back then," said Max's cousin, Curtis Harrison. "Guys from State College always had a game going on there. Max and I would get in and play for a few innings, sometimes more. Most of the time, it wasn't long though before he'd be ready to move on and want to go somewhere else."

Mr. Harrison was a good ball player, too, and wasn't always ready to leave when Max got antsy or irritated. "Somebody might've said the wrong thing to him or he'd just get the wrong thing stuck in his head and he'd lose his focus or get mad." Not wanting to make a bad situation worse, they'd load up their stuff and head for another field and another game.

Doak Field, the baseball facility named after Charles G. "Chick" Doak, the longtime (1924-1939) Wolfpack skipper, opened its gates in the spring of 1966. I have to believe that Max would have been there for that Grand Opening. If Max's cousin wasn't available and he couldn't find anyone else to take him to the big city, he would take the bus to the NC State College (later University) campus. Once there, he would find some unsuspecting sap to catch some of his attempts at breaking the sound barrier with a rawhide covered sphere. I would imagine that saps who could catch a 100+ mile per hour fastball would be few and far between. It kind of makes me wonder if Max ever killed anybody with his heater. I hope not.

Not far from NCSU was Devereux Meadow, home of the minor league Raleigh Capitals, among a few other team names over the years. Located just off Capital Boulevard, Devereux Meadow was a stop on the way to the majors for guys like Carl Yastrzemski, Ted Williams, Cliff Johnson, and many others.

Cliff who? Look him up.

Never mind. I'll tell you how I know about Cliff Johnson. Please pardon this diversion…

In the summer of 1970 I went so see my first professional baseball game at Devereux Meadow. Sometime in July, Wayne Perry, older brother of one of my neighborhood friends, took his brother Lynn, Robert Lee (not the famous one, even though "E" *is* his middle initial), and me to a night game. Lynn and I were pretty much on the same footing, but Robert still hadn't hit his growth spurt yet and was just this little redheaded kid who went with us. He was a little younger than us, but he loved to tag along wherever we went, so, there he was. He was a good kid, but annoying as trying put on a turtleneck sweater over a football helmet.

Three scenes from that game make the rounds through my mind quite often.

First and foremost, there was this absolutely, drop-dead, gorgeous girl there who kept walking by where we were sitting on the front row of the bleachers just past the dugout on the 1st base side. She appeared to be a few years older than us, but 15-year old guys would have to be dead to possibly care any less about such nonsense as age difference. She wouldn't tell us her name, but when we asked where she was from, she said, in the sweetest and most Southern Belle voice I'd ever heard, "Tick Bite, North Carolina."

Lynn and I were trying to be suave, debonair, and sophisticated to impress this young lady, but we were still just adolescent boys. When we heard her say that, we fell all over the bleachers, and if I dare say so, we laughed our asses off. Tick Bite? Really? The community of Lizard Lick is five miles outside of Zebulon, but Tick Bite? She made that shit up! Sorry, to the folks from Tick Bite, no offense. She stalked off and we figured that we had blown our chances with her, so we started focusing on the game. There were more important things going on like popcorn, peanuts, and Cracker Jacks.

Somewhere around the 5th or 6th inning, guess who came sauntering by us, smiling like a Cheshire cat, and carrying in her lithe and loving arms like a newborn baby, the now infamous Robert E-freaking Lee? None other than the lovely Miss Tick Bite 1970.

Some things just can't be explained.

I have to back up to the 1st or 2nd inning to tell about the second memory. There weren't a lot of people in the stands, perhaps three or four hundred, but it could have been five hundred for all I know. Lots of empty seats, though. At about this time, a bus pulled up outside the gate of the rightfield bleachers where we had entered the stadium and not far from were sitting. A crowd of about 15 or 20 grown-ups, men and women, disembarked, came in, and disbursed into the seats all around us. After a few minutes of checking them out, in the manner young boys are apt to do, Lynn and I noticed that something was not quite right with the newcomers. Some were rocking, some were conversing with themselves, and most were paying no attention whatsoever to the baseball game.

There was this one guy, though, who came in with them and he was focused on the game. He was standing somewhat in front of us at the fence beside the dugout and watching the game from ground level. I never got a look at his face, but I don't recall any other the other faces I saw that night either, except for Miss Tick Bite 1970, and her lovely image is forever etched upon my mind.

We looked questioningly at Wayne, who quietly and discreetly told us they were probably a group of patients from Dix Hill. He then explained about the state mental hospital a few miles away and mental illness in general, even though both of us knew a little about the subject.

Even now, as strongly as I want to recall the face of Max Mangum that night, it just isn't there. That would be just way too much for me to handle. This story is strange enough as it is.

Do I think Max was at that game in 1970? I do.

Do I think that was when our paths actually crossed for the first time? For some reason, I absolutely do. It was an unofficial path-crossing, though.

Some things just can't be explained.

Back to Cliff Johnson. We could tell by the crowd's reaction every time Cliff came to the plate that he was the stud on the team. The man. The stud man. He definitely hit the ball hard when he hit it, no question about that. Late in the game, he came to bat for what was more than likely going to be his final at-bat for the night.

Capital Boulevard ran parallel just beyond the left field fence and almost to center before it veered away gently to the left and toward downtown Raleigh. I don't recall the dimensions of Devereux Meadow, but it was fairly deep out toward left and center. Not Washington's old Griffith Stadium-deep, but deep. Johnson pulled one just foul out toward left that went out of the stadium and bounced between some cars passing by on Capital Boulevard.

The crowd came alive and was buzzing. We were buzzing, too.

"Did you see that?" I said.

"Wow! Straighten one out, Johnson!" Wayne yelled.

I poured out a handful of Cracker Jacks and passed the box to Lynn. "Straighten one out, Johnson," I said, echoing Wayne's request.

The pitcher was about to release the next pitch when Lynn pointed and said, "Watch this! He's gonna hit that truck!"

I looked to where he was pointing and an 18-wheeler was just clearing the left field corner of the stadium, heading downtown. I heard a loud crack, a couple of hundred screams, and then I watched that damn baseball as it went over the wall in the power alley between left and center. It carried way over the berm behind the fence and hit the back righthand side of that southbound 18-wheeler. How could I ever forget Cliff Johnson?

When he made it to the major leagues a year or two later and was traded to the Yankees, my Yankee fan friends would say, "Who the hell is Cliff Johnson?" and then I'd tell them about my encounter with the slugger when he was a minor league player. Yes, they looked at me kind of like how you're looking at this page right now. Tell the truth. Your eyes are slightly squinted, lips together in a half-smile, and disbelieving what you're reading. Am I right?

Some things just can't be explained.

I can easily see Max chomping at the rosin bag for a chance to get in there on the mound at Devereux Meadow and square off against Yaz or Ted "The Splendid Splinter" Williams or maybe even Cliff Johnson. I can also see him confused and disillusioned by the fact that he can't get in there and pitch against these guys. He knows he's got the stuff to sit them down, but no one will take him seriously. It doesn't take a doctorate to infer that something is not exactly kosher with the guy throwing BBs, talking to himself, and slamming his glove down in the dirt.

Also, just a few blocks away in downtown Raleigh is Johnson-Lambe Sporting Goods. "Max used to come in here all the time back in the 60s looking at new baseballs and gloves," said Phil Johnson, one of the principal owners of the store. He also formed a good relationship with Max during this time. His store was only a few short city blocks from Dorothea Dix Hospital, an easy walk for Max when he was a patient there.

"Every now and then when he came in, he'd talk some rube shopping here in the store into going out between the buildings to catch him. Never lasted very long though," smiled Mr. Johnson as the memory carried him back in time. "There was only about four or five feet between the brick buildings, just a very narrow alleyway. It didn't take long for Mr. Rube to figure out that if this guy happens to get the least bit wild, that fastball was liable to be the last thing he ever saw!" I laughed when I pictured one of Max's 100+ mile per hour fastballs ricocheting off the bricks of both buildings and coming to rest just inside and to the left of Mr. Rube's frontal lobe.

Then suddenly, I had a vision of that ball coming to rest in *my* frontal lobe and it didn't seem so funny anymore.

Mr. Johnson said it was obvious that all Max wanted to do was pitch in game somewhere, so he vowed to help him out if he ever got the chance. One day Mr. J overheard a couple of his frequent customers chatting about an upcoming baseball tournament. The two black men said that their traveling team was heading to Myrtle Beach the following weekend for the 3-day event. Mr. Johnson asked if they could use another pitcher and they both answered with a resounding "Yes!" Mr. Johnson hooked them up with Max a few days later and off they went the next Friday on a trip to South Carolina for a weekend of baseball bliss.

"Didn't happen, though," said Mr. Johnson. "Not the way it was supposed to." Deep inside, I had a feeling that it wasn't going to pan out, either. Mr. Johnson continued, "The guys said there were five of them and Max riding in one car and about ten miles out of Raleigh, Max started acting strangely." Mr. Johnson had told them that Max had a little problem, but they said they needed another pitcher. How bad could the little problem be?

Apparently, really bad.

"One guy said Max was kind of quiet the first fifteen minutes," Mr. Johnson added, "then he began looking around at the guys in the car and starting singing some crazy song about monkeys swingin' in the trees." Mr. Johnson just shook his head at the memory and finished by saying, "They thought it would be best if they just took him back to the place where they'd picked him up."

I cringed when I considered adding this part to the story, but it happened and I'm going to tell it like it is.

Life ain't always pretty.

Raise your hand if you have never in your life said, done, or thought anything of a racist nature…

Ok, yes. Good. You there, in the robe! With the beard and the halo. That's what I figured. I applaud You. The rest of us? We have to live and learn.

Former New York Yankee pitcher Tommy Byrne moved to Wake Forest after he retired from baseball in 1957 and Max would visit with him regularly. Mr. Byrne helped out with youth baseball in the area, but also sponsored a couple of major league tryouts and that was right up Max's alley. In the mid-60's, Max was in his mid-30's and way past his chance for signing any contracts to play major league baseball, but there was no need to tell Max that he was too old. It wouldn't have done any good anyway.

The steady St. Louis Cardinals catcher Ted Simmons and former Milwaukee Braves slugger Joe Adcock are both credited with the quote, "Trying to sneak a fastball past Hank Aaron is like trying to sneak the sunrise past a rooster." I love that quote. I'd like to coin my own quote here and say that, "Trying to sneak a major league tryout past Max Mangum is like trying to sneak a fastball past Hank Aaron at sunrise with a rooster sitting on his shoulder."

Well, it needs work, but you know what I mean.

Max attended a couple of Tommy Byrnes' tryout camps, that's for certain, but there is no way of knowing just how many major league tryouts he may have crashed in his lifetime. I remember his sister, Mrs. Davis, saying that Max had gone to some tryouts in Raleigh but most of the time he was teased a lot by some of the younger guys who were trying out. I'm sure they were a little envious of his blazing fastball. If they could get him out of there, maybe they would have a better chance of getting noticed. Kids, even kids in their late teens and early twenties, can be very cruel.

Mrs. Davis said that Max told her on several occasions that the scouts had told him that if he were 18 or 19 or even 20 years old, they would have offered him a contract on the spot.

Problem is, none of that age nonsense has ever mattered to Max and I found solid – rock solid – proof that Max was a pro baseball tryout hound, but I can't reveal it just yet.

Hang in there.

Chapter 13

WHO WOULDN'T BE DEPRESSED to discover that the establishment that issued you a paycheck on a regular basis was going belly up? I was certainly depressed, but what depressed me even more was the thought of having to go out and try to find another job where I had to kiss ass every day to make a living. I wasn't even kissing ass for myself. I was always kissing ass for somebody else and having to grin like a Cheshire cat the whole time I was doing it! *That'll be $134.95, sir. Thank you very much. Y'all come back and see us now, hear?*

Over the years, I had given little thought to doing something different, so I had no idea what else I might do to earn a living. I was at an age where, let's face it, people don't change careers at thirty-seven. I'd had my opportunities and I'd let them slip away. I also had a few weeks to think about it, though.

Writing the first part of this story for the magazine put me back in touch with a part of me that had lain dormant for many years. I'd always enjoyed writing and this story had turned into an incredible adventure for me, figuratively and literally. If I ever had a spare minute or two, I was always tweaking 'The Phantom of the Bullpen' and had accumulated about twenty versions and revisions. I felt in my heart that this story was special and I was very diligent in trying to get it exactly right, exactly as it happened, while still mixing in some of my own misadventures.

Pam read the story one evening (definitely not this version) in early June of 1992 and suggested rather calmly and from deep left field that I should go to college.

"Huh? For what, Babe?" I asked, because I'm sometimes clueless and really didn't know why she would say something so utterly absurd.

She dropped the story on my desk and said, "I don't know, so you can teach writing and coach baseball. You know, realize your dream, that sort of thing."

"We can't afford –

"Yes, we can."

"But what about –

"You can attend classes at night at Nash Community College. They have a college transfer program."

"But I can't –

I shut myself up that time. The clouds of confusion and doubt rolled away and suddenly I could see the light. Here and now I have a chance to do something I've been wanting and longing and needing to do for two decades: get that sheepskin so I can teach and coach and make a living doing it. Talk about a dream come true. And all I had to do to accomplish this fantastic feat was to get out of my own way.

Max, on the other hand, has been, and there's no better way to put this or I would, working his ass off every day possible for forty-five years trying to do something he will *never* get a chance to do: pitch in the major leagues.

In my mind I could see Max out in his bullpen, blowing strike after strike through that hanging tire, day after day, week after week, year after year. Then I saw him pause in his delivery. Time stood still again and I could hear nothing, not even the crickets.

He looked directly at me and the expression on his face was screaming, "Whatcha gonna do? At least one of us can get something out of this."

"I can do this, Babe," I said proudly.

"I know you can," Pam said sweetly. "And you can take out the trash, too."

Well, alrighty then.

I entertained this exciting idea for a few days. I tried to see myself going to college again, minus the drugs, the drinking, and the wild women. Well, there went a lot of the excitement, but I was still excited in a different way. If I can pull this off, maybe I can really make a difference in the world, or at least in my corner of it.

Jean-Marc Savory from the ZPRD called me about a week after I lost my job. Keep in mind that the very day that Dennis Equipment Company went out of business the previous week, I had declared and committed to play our Father's Day tournament games at the Zebulon Community Park and at Zebulon High School, my alma mater, which had been a middle school since 1990. I made a hundred phone calls that day to make it official and inform everyone who needed to be informed. If I'm not mistaken, and I'm not, the very first of those phone calls went to Mr. Savory about securing the fields. See if you can make some sense of this conversation:

"Allen? Jean-Marc. Good news! Mr. Bryant wants to talk to you about possibly using Five County Stadium for your tournament," he said.

I said without too much emotion, certainly not the emotion I was feeling, "It's too late, Jean-Marc. You know that."

It was like he didn't even hear me, as if he were reading from a script. He then said, "Mr. Bryant says he can meet with you sometime next week, but he wants you to understand that the Mudcats and the stadium administrators do *NOT*" (and he really over-stressed the *NOT* part) "want to be associated with tractor-pulls and rodeos and things of this nature," Jean-Marc told me.

The bullshit was coming in fast and furious from deep, deep left field and I felt completely powerless to stop it. What *in the hell* is this man talking about? And why is he the middleman in a three-ring circus that's already folded up the tents and left town? The tournament was less than two weeks away! Tractor-pulls? Rodeos?

Check, please!

In my mind, I went off on a tirade with a little hastily prepared speech of my own.

"Jean-Marc, all we wanted to do was give some old timers a chance to play some ball on a nice field. The powers that be call it a stadium, and it will be one day; I've seen the plans. But right now, it's just a nice baseball field with a nice big wall in the outfield and some Mickey Mouse bleachers thrown up along the foul lines and a grandstand behind home plate. That 10-foot high chain link fence surrounding the place is there to keep the no-paying riff-raff out and the high-rolling riff-raff in. A few of the guys in our league are former

major league and minor league players, but most are guys like me: guys who were damn good ballplayers, but never made it past all the expectations for a thousand different reasons. I just wanted some of the guys to feel the 'big time' again and I wanted some of us to feel it for the first time. But that's all right, Jean-Marc, because I know you somehow got stuck in the middle of this nonsense and it's not your fault and it's really no big deal. If we never touch on the subject again, well, that will be just fine with me because it's over. Let It Be," is what I *wanted* to say.

What I actually said was, "Thank you kindly, but we're going to stick with our current arrangements."

You don't burn bridges if you can't swim.

Chapter 14

I saw Max Mangum for the third or possibly the fourth time in my life on Sunday, less than a week before the Father's Day tournament was to begin the following Friday night. He had hitched a ride to the high school in Wake Forest where we were playing the Dodgers' sister team, the Cardinals. We invited Max to sit with us in our dugout. I told him that he was starting next Saturday morning in the Father's Day tournament and he went ballistic.

He warmed up on the sidelines and even did some sprints. I hate to admit it, but he runs a lot better than some of the guys on our team. (Don't tell them I said that.) I had my camera with me and sneaked a few shots of Max while he wasn't looking. As I took the last one, he turned and gave me that funny little smile again.

Five of the twenty-four pictures I took that day were of Max. Every picture on the roll was perfect and clear as a bell, except for the five of Max. Each one of those photographs sported a big, dark, fuzzy blob outlined in red right in the middle of the print.

Don't ask me. I don't know what the problem was and it was getting to the point where I didn't really care. If it was not meant for me to get a good photograph of Max, then I certainly wasn't going to keep forcing the issue. It was as though some unknown entity was interfering every time I tried to get his picture.

From right to left along the dugout: Alicia Fulmer (Bobby's wife), Randy Pearce, Max in the flesh in the weird glow, Walt Perry, and Patrick Pearce (Welton's son).

Max was standing right there, just looking at me. What IS that? Would I have taken the picture if I'd seen something like that in front of me?

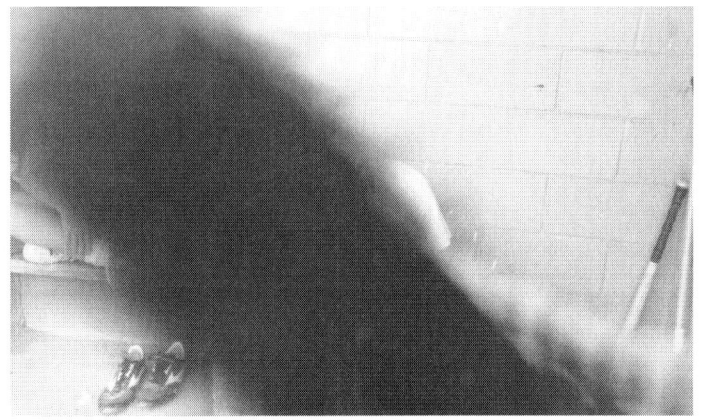

Again, Max was just sitting there, looking right into the camera.

Right to left: Randy, Max evading the blob, Walt, and Welton.

Hell, maybe he's a vampire and doesn't register a reflection in mirrors, either. Na. Max didn't have all that many teeth and none of them were pointy anyway. What if he's the one who's being punished or toyed with here, and not me? What if I was unsuspectingly interfering with some kind of supernatural mumbo-jumbo voodoo curse stuff and I was just one more little butt-in away from getting zapped into a turd or something?

Do I really believe any of these nonsense explanations? No, I don't think so, but like I said before, I don't take careless chances either. I knew from watching television that when you mess with things you don't understand, you end up with star-billing in a scary movie, and I'm just not cut out for that kind of excitement.

The big weekend finally rolled around. Jameson and I drove to Wake Forest and picked up Max bright and early that Saturday morning for his start at the Joe O'Neal Baseball Complex on the campus of Zebulon Middle School. It's not really called that, but that's what I'm calling it right now. Mr. Joe O'Neal was the hard-working custodian at the school for many years and kept both the inside and the outside looking topnotch. This little piece of superfluous recognition is for him.

For Max Mangum, it was a baseball game about five decades in the making. We arrived on campus just in time to help my teammates drag the infield and redo the foul lines and batter's boxes.

Welcome to the Big Time, Max.

Max didn't miss a beat. He tossed his glove into the dugout, pushed up the sleeves on his nylon jacket, and jumped right in. He helped Walt and Randy with the batter's boxes while Welton and I reset the bases and did some raking. A few minutes later, I looked up from the rake to see what Max was getting into. I saw him walk over to the line machine, reach in with both hands and scoop out some powder.

He walked over to an area in front of the visitor's dugout and proceeded to lay down an on-deck circle that, from where I was standing, looked a whole lot like the five-sided one that freaked me out at Durham Athletic Park one evening eight months ago. Max finished and then did the *odd*est thing. He clapped the dust from his hands five times, then wiped them off on his pants three times, and then spit once – right into the middle of his multi-cornered on-deck circle. He looked over at me standing there with my mouth open and gave me that damn smile again.

Shit. Now I know he's a warlock!

On my way across the field to retrieve my glove from the dugout, I caught a glimpse of the Grand Canyon, in all its natural beauty, out of the corner of my left eye. A few steps later, I stopped and it hit me. The Grand Canyon is not in Zebulon! I peeked back over my shoulder at the pitcher's mound and saw a quarry that had been spiked out in front of the pitcher's plate during the two Friday night games.

I pitched from that same mound when I was in high school, so I knew the thing was at least twenty-five years old and had been the victim of absolutely no maintenance since 1989, the last year of Zebulon High. Calling it a mound was doing it a favor. The many years of rainfall had eroded that once majestic pile of clay into a six-inch irregular hump that almost spanned the whole middle of the infield.

I honestly believe the bottom of that pit in front of the rubber was lower than the rest of the infield. The guys who pitched in the two games played there Friday night must have been shelled pretty hard judging from the size of that foxhole. I asked Max what he thought about the crater and he confirmed my suspicions. Max said, "Musta been one of them meteorites." He didn't seem to think it would affect his pitching, but I was worried enough for both of us anyway.

I said to Max, "I can put some more dirt in there, Max, if you want me to. Do you think it's going to be a problem?" I know how I am always very particular about the mound, how everything has to be just perfect. Not Mark 'The Bird' Fidrych perfect, but close. I hated those pitchers who would come out and just start digging a trench with their spikes in front of the rubber *before* they ever threw their first warm-up pitch. What the hell? I never understood that. If that were the ideal surface for effective pitching, wouldn't it have been designed that way to begin with? I understand about getting more leverage with your leg to push off toward the plate on the delivery of the pitch but defacing the mound like that always seemed like cheating to me.

Max said, "You been to my place."

Indeed I had. Max didn't have a mound or a pitching rubber or even a rosin bag. His pitching area was just a small rise in the land and a tire hanging in a tree.

"So this is not going to be a problem, right?" I asked, almost hopefully.

"Let's just play ball!" Max roared.

And play we did.

A combination of several factors, I believe, contributed to Max's mediocre performance in the game. The basement apartment he had to pitch from, for one thing, was a royal pain in the arse. Trying to compensate for the difference could have been why he was so consistently a little high out of the strike zone. Secondly, I have since measured the dimensions at Max's bullpen at Shade Stadium and discovered that he throws regularly from a distance of slightly more than sixty-two feet, instead of the regulation sixty feet, six inches.

Those two extra feet and that crater could have been the difference between the eleven base-on-balls he issued and the forty-four knee-high strikes that might have been. He just couldn't get it down. Also, this was the first time in nearly fifty years that Max had faced live batters in a game situation. He had the right to be a little tight.

I shouldn't say anything negative about the guys on the other team, but I'm going to do just that. I, too, may have reacted with some indignation the way they did if someone had put some ancient old timer on the mound to pitch to us, but I don't think I would have been so cold and so obvious about it. These guys thought it was some kind of a joke until they saw that, despite his awkward appearance, old grandpa could push the pill. While warming up, Max was drawing dust from Neal Narron's mitt, but it was easy to see that he was very uncomfortable on that horrid mound.

I don't think the first four batters swung at a single pitch. Max was throwing the high, hard, stinky cheese, but it was just a little too high, and the umpire was calling them close, as he should. Baseball is a game of inches, too.

Some of my teammates were getting a little frustrated at this point. It's tough, damn near impossible, to stay focused and be ready to play defense in the field when the pitcher is walking everybody. Your mind starts to drift and the next thing you know, you're under your truck changing the oil when something very hard moving very fast whizzes by your head and you know it wasn't an oil filter.

One of the guys, I know which one but I'm not saying, caught my attention and drew a dagger-like finger across his neck in an effort to get me to pull Max out of the game. Perhaps it was unfair of me to expect everyone to go along with this thing. I'd come up with this tournament for all of us, but this one game was for Max. They knew that, but frustration leads to impatience, and I understood their predicament.

Yes, I understood, but I let Max pitch.

I was saddled with uncomfortable task of acting as manager that game. Usually, we just made out a line-up card before the game started and one of the guys not starting would volunteer to be 'manager' and work everybody, himself included, into the game at some point. No real managing going on by one guy with all the brains. It took all our brains sometimes just to come up with a *bad* decision.

Max tallied a couple of strikeouts with his blistering fastball, but the bad guys scored a bunch in the second due to more walks. Max continued to struggle. He was still throwing it too high upstairs in the third, so I had to take a trip to the mound. I met catcher Neal Narron there and asked him, "Whadya think, Neal?"

"He's throwin' the hell out of it, but he's got to bring it down a little," Neal said, examining his red left palm.

"Gotta bring it down, Max," I said, directing my attention to him. "Is your arm ok?"

"My arm's fine," Max said. "But there's a ever-lovin' double criminal back there somewhere." He gestured toward the backstop and the two small sets of bleachers beyond it and said, "And he's stealin' my 'lectricity!"

I didn't know what to say, even though I had heard Max say that same thing before, so I said, "Well then, reach in there and pull his damn fuse."

Max thought that was funny as hell and told me to go on back to the dugout. I was only happy to oblige.

Although we were beaten soundly by the team from Southern Pines, 13-8, it was evident that Max had a great time. Thanks to my teammates, we were able to make at least a small part of his dream come true. We had a team picture taken after the game and this bears repeating, so I will: I don't think any of us stood any prouder than Max Mangum.

The Zebulon Pirates: Back row (l-r) Max Mangum, Ricky Strickland, Stacey Overman, Kirk Pollard, Scott Peele, Randy Pearce. Front row (l-r) Allen White, Bobby Follmer, Welton Pearce, Roger Wood, Neal Narron.

Chapter 15

To THIS DAY (present day, whatever it may be), Max will still have me pegged as a scout for the Pittsburgh Pirates. That was his first impression of me and it has never wavered. He also believed there was a worldwide conspiracy to keep him out of the major leagues, and to him, it actually looked that way, and I could see his point.

Max called me on the telephone from his sister's house in mid-August of 1992. I could tell that he was frustrated. He asked me, "What do I have to do?" and "Ain't age discrimination against the law?" I didn't have worthy answers so I didn't offer any. I tried to get one of the two Wake Forest teams to pick him up the following season, but neither did. Of course, there was, and still is, hope.

Later in the year, sometime in September, I was making my way to my seat at the final home game of the Carolina Mudcats second season when I was approached by one of their public relations representatives. Sandy was her name, I think, but don't hold me to that. Dressed in her red satin Mudcats jacket and dark slacks, she flashed a thousand-watt smile as she touched my arm to get my attention.

She asked me, "Do you happen to know an elderly gentleman from this area who may be a wee bit senile?"

About six or seven of my closest and craziest friends crossed my mind immediately, but I kept my cards close. "Maybe," I said, noncommittally.

She continued, "Anyway, this fellow is telling everyone here at the Mudcats' office that he can pitch the Pittsburgh Pirates into the World Series in October if he could just get a tryout."

Well, that narrowed down the list of suspects.

Max Mangum strikes again.

I said, "No shit? You guys give him a look?"

"No, not really," she said, blushing. Then she droned on for a minute or so about how she thought he was a really nice man, and she thought he was pitiful, but he had mentioned my name as a reference when he called, and that's why she was asking me.

I could feel my old heart bending but it refused to break this time, and breaking with personal tradition, I actually gave some thought to my response before replying.

I thought about the man who had recently showed me that the only difference between himself and the Nolan Ryans of the world were the uncontrollable and sometimes unfortunate breaks in life. I thought about the man who had helped me slow down and smell a rose or two lately. It was because of him that I had even considered going back to college to get what I needed to fulfill a dream that I had given up on long, long ago. I thought deeply, but quickly, about a lot of things before I finally spoke.

"Yes, Ma'am. I do know this gentleman. He's a good friend of mine." I answered. "His name is Max Mangum, but I'll tell you one thing about him straight up and serious."

She asked, "What's that?"

"The only thing pitiful about him is that he's telling you the truth."

(This was another one of the endings to this story that just didn't pan out.)

Chapter 16

IN JANUARY OF 1993, I enrolled for night classes at Nash Community College in Rocky Mount. Although I was twenty years behind on a four-year plan, I had the support of my wife and kids and an optimistic outlook that had no limits.

At the same time, I took a job for peanuts and benefits with the Wake County Public School System as a teacher assistant in special programs at Zebulon Middle School. Yes, the benefits were exceptional and the peanuts were a hell of a lot better than no peanuts, but the best part was that I no longer hated going to work. Quite the opposite. Getting up every day and going to work and not having much of a clue as to what might happen at any given moment was *exciting*. Until this minute, 'exciting' and 'work' were two words I'd never used in the same sentence. (And now I see that I've done it two sentences in a row.) When my job was done at school, I headed off to school myself!

Life was good!

At ZMS, my old high school, I worked with many new people, but there were a few remnants still around from my era. The school secretary, Ruby Watkins, was still there keeping the administrative part of the school running smoothly. Joe O'Neal was still the head custodian and keeping everything else up and running. Jessie (Ives) Dixon was still teaching there. She was a first or second year French teacher at ZHS my senior year. I had her for study hall, where I was majoring in mischief and seeking a minor in mayhem. Needless to say, when I saw her there on the first day of my new job, I was so ashamed. I'd hate to think what she might have been thinking about me being there as a teacher.

Well, there goes the Wake County Public School System.

A few of the folks I went to school with were now teaching there, and one kid I had coached in Mighty Mite football, Eddie Kemp, had just been hired to teach social studies and coach the football team. What the hell? Am I getting old or something?

After school was out for the day, I jumped into my truck and headed for college. Weird. Weird, but fun.

I met a lot of interesting people at Nash Community College. Dr. Evelyn Mattern was my first English professor and she helped me tremendously with the nuts and bolts of writing (I hope), but her endless encouragement was especially helpful. She was a nun, or used to be a nun at one time, or just wanted to become a nun. I'm not sure which rumor to believe. She had a good heart, so I guess that explains why she never lost hope in me. Nuns don't give up on *anyone.*

Another of my professors was Jay Peacock, a heck of a nice guy, but anybody is going to be cool with a name like Jay Peacock. He was a history and geography guy, like me, and we connected on many levels. I think it may have been Jay's letter of reference that got me into North Carolina State a few years later.

I have to tell this story. It's just too funny to pass up.

Bill O'Boyle has a funny name and he was my English Literature professor in my third semester there, but that's not really the funny part. He awakened me to the classics when we read 'The Canterbury Tales' by Geoffrey Chaucer. What I thought was going to be as boring as watching whales migrate turned out to be some of the funniest stuff I'd ever read. Professor O'Boyle also sold beer at Five County Stadium when the Mudcats were in town.

What a guy!

I probably shouldn't tell this, but once again, I think I've gone too far to bail out.

O'Boyle got me good one evening in class. The previous night, I had literally stayed up until dawn that morning working on a Chaucer essay that was due for his class that evening. Finishing up, I grabbed a shower, got dressed, and went to work at ZMS until 4pm. I then drove the 25 miles to NCC, proofreading my essay the whole way there.

I know, I know. But traffic was light.

My first class that evening, biology, went on a walking field trip around the campus, out in the woods, and finally down in a damn swamp, but it was a stumbling field trip for me. I was fading fast. By the time I shuffled into Bill O'Boyle's class, I was dragging a heavy load and nodding on my feet. I could literally feel my shit closing down.

Determined to wake myself up, I took the first seat in the row directly in front of the professor's desk. My posture may have portrayed intense interest, but from the neck up, I was struggling. Every time I blinked my eyes, it took me nearly five seconds to pry them back open again. Sleep Come Free Me.

O'Boyle, not sleep, came in like his pants were on fire and he had no intention of putting them out. He dropped his stuff on his desk, strutted briskly around to the front of it, and hopped up on the left corner, about a foot from my desk. I tried to shrug off my sluggishness and perk up a little bit. Reaching down deep inside, I pulled out some fresh resolve and it worked. For about one blink.

As I was fading off into Never Neverland again, I heard Mr. O'Boyle say, "Tonight, ladies and gentlemen, we are going to take an intimate, in-depth, up-close, and in-your-face look," and he paused here and looked directly at me, "at the Wife of Bath's Tale."

Total silence in the room.

I knew damn well what he was talking about, but the way he said 'tale' just totally destroyed my mind and then my discipline. He said 'tale' but I heard 'tail.' And I tried so hard not to laugh. For a few seconds, my head just bobbed up and down and my stomach got hard as a rock from trying to hold it in.

And then the floodgates buckled. I snorted about three times, thinking that I could cut it off, recover, and hold it in. Nope. I heard some other students starting to laugh and the floodgates were obliterated. I totally lost it. Even Bill O'Boyle was laughing. The madness lasted a few minutes while everybody tried to get their shit back together.

Perhaps I was the catalyst that got the laughing started, but I'm sorry. I don't think I was the only one who heard 'tail' instead of 'tale.' The way he said the word threw me for a loop in my weakened state and resistance was not even a distant choice.

Professor O'Boyle took off his glasses, wiped the tears from his eyes, and asked me, "Allen, what was so funny about what I said?" He was still laughing.

I told him the truth.

I said, "You've already told us several times what a slut the woman is, sir. I don't think I want to get that close to her."

And then we laughed some more.

I studied psychology at NCC under Dr. David West, a truly interesting man who hailed from Michigan. I say interesting because he reminded me of three different celebrities: He resembled Charles Durning in appearance, his voice sounded like one of Jonathan Winters' voices, and his dry wit and mannerisms reminded me of Paul Lynde.

My fourth and final semester at Nash, Dr. West talked me into taking a computer course which I thought was going to be Intro to Computers 101 for Idiots or something like that, because that's what I was and that's what I needed. I had just recently discovered that there's quite a difference between a typewriter and a computer.

What the class actually turned out to be was Programming in Turbo C++ (plus, plus), whatever the hell that means. I took the damn course and still can't tell you anything about it. I should have gotten an F--(minus, minus), but he gave me a D instead, for Dumbass, no doubt. I still don't know how he psyched me into taking that class.

One of my elective classes that same semester was The Fundamentals of Golf, so I always had my $100 set of yard sale golf clubs in the back of my car. I hate to admit to this, but there were a couple of days I just wasn't in the Turbo C++ mood and I put my ass into turbo-charged mode and skipped that binary bullshit and played some golf. And I hate golf. I'm more than happy to admit, though, that skipping class again felt *goooood*.

I hadn't seen Max since the tournament in June of '92, but I found myself thinking about him often. For my Comp 101 class, I got a chance to write another short story about him. I called it "The Story About the Man in the Story" and my classmates and my professor loved it, especially when I bragged that the real story, "Phantom of the Bullpen", was going to be published in a magazine.

In that essay, I was able to write basically a complete summary of the whole story, fleshing out some of the things I'd simply hinted at and then skipped over in the original. Also, for Psyche 101, I got to write (make up, basically, but don't tell Dr. West) a case study on Max that received, oddly enough, a grade of 101. Apparently, I too, have the gift of bull.

I was beginning to think I may very well be obsessed with this man, this phantom, this baseball-throwing machine I'd met by accident when all the stars and planets and moons and asteroids and comets and space junk had lined up in a certain geometric pattern *Across the Universe* and made the tumblers click and allowed the cogs to mesh.

That sentence, in itself, may be proof enough right there.

The excuse I conveniently used for continuing to write about Max was convenience. We did a lot of writing and I wrote essays on many different subjects, but if the assignment allowed for some kind of connection to Max, I made it and ran with it. One of the first things Dr. Mattern taught us in Comp class was 'write about what you know' and you can't go wrong. I felt that this was sound advice and acted accordingly.

Am I obsessed? Am I crazy? I didn't think so, but usually those who truly are crazy never think so, either. I sure as hell didn't know if I was obsessed or crazy, but I made a note to myself to ask myself these tough and serious questions again later.

Uh oh.

My friend Welton and I dropped in on Max in May that year on our first trip to Wake Forest to play the Dodgers that summer. We had about an hour to kill before the game, so we headed off for Shade Stadium and a serious game of catch. The three of us tossed the ball around for a bit, and Max said, "I'd like to air it out now, if I could."

We took turns catching Max and my second baseman was still just as impressed with him as I was.

"Easy, Max," Welton begged. "I don't weigh but about a buck fifty."

Max laughed and said, "You gonna need a anchor then."

Max had that quality all hard-throwing pitchers have: the ability to make a baseball look like a pea. Talk about watching the ball all the way to your glove. The only other option was to watch it all the way to your face, and you'd only get to do that once. Throwing with Max was an intense lesson in the basic fundamentals for catching a baseball. Keep your eye on the ball, period. Anything else could get you killed. After thirty or so pitches to each of us, my hand was swelling up in my glove, but it was Welton who said he'd had enough, not me.

"I can't take another round of that shit, Allen. Let's get outta here. He's killin' me," Welton whispered. He started to give me ten but pulled his throbbing left hand back quickly and said, "I'll have to give you a rain check on the other five."

We bade Max farewell and lit off for the game at Wake Forest-Rolesville High School.

If Max had the stuff to make the baseball look like a pea, the guy pitching for the Dodge Boys that day had the unfortunate ability to make the baseball look like a beach ball against a stiff ocean breeze. Welton and I knew that catching Max was the reason both of us were zeroed in and banging the ball off that chain link fence in the outfield all afternoon. All Welton said on the way home was, "We ought to go see Max before *every* ball game." He said it about twelve times, giving me a soft 'air' five each time.

In August I turned over the operations of the Zebulon Pirates to Walt Perry, our third baseman. But I still wanted to play baseball, which was my whole reason behind creating the team. What? I told you I was selfish. It was the endless phone calls and having to coordinate everything that was causing me some nagging little problems. Yes, there is a double entendre near the end of the previous sentence, but it would be beneath me to point it out.

My classes were getting tougher and I needed to be studying instead of playing baseball, or *so said my wife!* I was sure that I could do it all and then some, but I'd been wrong before, and after all, which is more important? My career? Or playing some stupid kids' game? I mean, I had to get my priorities straight. I'm all grown up now, damn it; I'm a man!

(Imagine, if you will, me singing the Spencer Davis Group's I'm a Man, *because I can't sing. At all.)*

"Please don't make me quit playing baseball! I'll stay up and study all night long," I pleaded.

Pam informed me, "You already stay up all night studying."

I considered this truth carefully and said, "I can study during lunch every day!" and patted my stomach, indicating I might also lose some of that weight she was always harping about, I mean, lovingly reminding me about.

She smiled and said mockingly in *my* native dialect, "We both know *that* ain't gonna happen, now don't we?"

"OK, OK, OK," I said, giving in. "I guess this season will be my fare-

"Fair enough," Pam inserted. "And don't forget to mow the lawn."

"-well tour…"

"Today."

Well now. Way to go, Allen, I was thinking to myself again. *By George, that sure turned out like we wanted it to, didn't it? That's the way to stand up on your hind legs and beg like a man.*

Again, as much as I didn't want to admit it, Pam was right. I always knew that I'd found Mrs. Right when I met her, I just didn't know her first name was Always. I'm sorry. That's an old joke and a low blow, but sometimes you just don't have anything else left in the old arsenal. Pam was exactly right and I just didn't want to admit it.

There's no need to say that my relationship with my wife was a bit strained. Even if a thousand things were going right, there was always that one negative thing that tended to dominate the proceedings. Maybe all couples go through the same thing, but the very idea of arguing about something that was absolutely senseless, useless, and unworthy of attention just seemed absurd to me. I also had to learn from my wife that what I thought were 'arguments' were in reality 'discussions' of some sort. See, even that statement right there begs me to argue, I mean discuss, its validity.

Words. Don't'cha just love 'em?

In no way, shape, or form am I saying that our constant points of contention were Pam's fault. I confess to being at least one-half the problem. But the only thing both of us were really at fault for is being who we were. Pam helped me change some things in my life and for that, I will always be thankful and grateful. She was a major factor in helping me kick most of the nastiest of my bad habits. She's at least partially responsible for my transformation from wild, long-haired hippie to model citizen. Well, maybe not 'model citizen' but something closer to the norm. I do have to give credit where credit is due: Pam domesticated me.

Please understand that I loved my wife with all my heart. Pam is a wonderful person. To our children, she was the absolute best mother in the world. She taught me how to be a good parent, because I had no idea how it was supposed to be done. I didn't grow up in the average American home with a mom and a dad, 2.3 children, and a chocolate lab. Since I lacked a blueprint for this facet of life, I went with Pam's.

After a few years, though, I couldn't always agree with everything in her plan, and that's when most of our problems were born. Instead of working on the problems, we pushed them to the backburner and focused on raising our kids in what was quickly becoming a very challenging world. The only downside to leaving things unsettled on the backburner too long is that sometimes you burn down your house.

It was sometime in September when we played in Wake Forest again. Alone this time, except for my camcorder, I went by to see Max after another rout of the pitcher-less Dodgers. How utterly ironic. I stood there, playing catch with a man who probably could have redefined major league pitching from the late 40's, through the 50'and 60's, and possibly on into the 70's, 80's and early 90's! I mean, damn. He still threw the ball (at age 64) as well as a lot of the guys currently in the pros. It was a bitter, terribly bitter pill of irony that I had a tough time swallowing.

The best pitcher to ever come out of the town of Zebulon was Earl Bunn. Earl was a senior and I was a freshman on the last baseball team at Wakelon High School in the spring of 1970. I don't have any idea how good a pitcher Max was when he was in his late teens or early twenties, but at sixty-five, he was throwing the baseball basically on the same raw skill level as my one-time teammate, Earl the Pearl, was throwing it in the 1970s. As good a pitcher as I was, or thought I was, both Max and Earl were a little beyond my skill level and it's almost sacrilegious to even put myself in the same sentence with them.

Earl was the dominating pitcher in our conference. After graduating high school and a 2-year stint in the military, he dominated at Methodist College in Fayetteville, North Carolina from 1974 through 1977. The following is an excerpt from the website of Methodist's baseball program, under the Hall of Fame section:

> *Earl Bunn played baseball for the Monarchs from 1974-*
> *1977 and was the first Methodist baseball player to be selected*
> *NCAA Division III All-American, an honor which he received*
> *twice. Bunn, whose jersey was retired in 1997, still holds the*
> *Methodist College record for career wins (43), career starts*
> *(56), and career ERA (1.72).*

I also gleaned from the site the fact that Earl had five shut outs and threw fourteen complete games in 1976. He was inducted into the school's Hall of Fame in 2000. I was informed by a long-time friend, Rick Rogers, who also played alongside Earl in high school, that Methodist College celebrates "Earl Bunn Day" every year.

Baseball is a sport of stories, legends, and rumors. I've heard this next particular story, or legend, or rumor from three or four different places and people, and even though I have no way to verify it, I'm going to share it, nonetheless. Sometimes you just have to take that leap of faith.

During the summer, most of the colleges and universities in North Carolina participate in summer league play for their baseball programs. During one of Earl's summers at Methodist College, they had the privilege of squaring off against the University of North Carolina at Chapel Hill, a big-time Division I team, in a doubleheader. I was never able to get any of the finer details, but the big takeaway was that Earl Bunn beat Carolina *both games*!

The way I understand it, Earl came in to pitch in relief in the fourth inning of the first game to earn the win and then started and finished the second game, which was also won by Methodist. I wish I knew more about this event, but I don't. Do I believe it? Hell, yes I do.

Earl Bunn was an Ironman.

Max never got the chance to accomplish anything on the baseball field and any accomplishments I may have had on the field are restricted to youth league and high school, plus some good performances with the Pirates. With this story, I hope that Max goes down in the annals of baseball history as one of, if not *the*, greatest 'shoulda-been, coulda-been, and woulda-been' pitchers of all time. It would only be fair.

Back at Shade Stadium, Max "aired it out" again for about thirty minutes and my hand was reaching that comfortably numb stage. My legs, however, were cramping up, so I was happy when Max said, "Wanna see my move to first?"

Over the course of the next fifteen minutes, Max showed me his pick-off move to first, second, and even to third, about three times each. It was difficult to judge without a runner, and the distance may have been off a foot or two in either direction, but he could've picked off my fat ass with no problem. His move was silky smooth, quick, and deceptive.

He'd bring the ball up to his chest just like his regular abbreviated windup and give a little sigh. I can clearly remember seeing him begin his move, but before I could analyze it or figure out what the hell he was doing, the ball would be in my glove. All I could do was just give a little phantom swipe at the imaginary runner lunging in a losing attempt to get back to the base safely.

"Yo, Max. How 'bout a few minutes of video? It's just for me. I want to-

"You gonna show it to them big boys and get me a tryout?" Max interrupted.

I hung *my* head this time and said, "If it were possible, Max, I would have already done it." I wish I could have been a scout for the Pirates – or anybody. I would gladly, proudly go to bat for this man and try to get him signed. It would be a novelty, sure, on the Eddie Gael scale (but larger), and probably wouldn't have lasted very long, but what the hell does? I'd give him his shot.

Max absolutely, positively refused to let me record his pick-off moves. He must have a patent on them or something. He did, however, allow me to get about four minutes of priceless video of him throwing some heat, and a few seconds of Shade Stadium, including the gazebo and the tire hanging from the rope. At least now, if someone doesn't believe my story about the phantom, I can finally prove it – in living color. I hope. He had lost about 5 to 8-miles per hour off his fastball by this time and he was having a little trouble catching the ball when I tossed it back to him, but don't be surprised if you see this scene in a movie someday.

With my past track record of getting Max on any kind of film, I began to wonder and worry about how this possibly priceless bit of footage might turn out. I won't say I was scared to watch it the first time, but that doesn't mean it's not true. What if there'd been no one in the scene but me, squatting there in the woods, and catching fastball after fastball that seemed to leap from another dimension. A wrinkle in reality. The birds chirping loudly, the squirrels chattering noisily, and me saying, "Good pitch, Max. Damn good pitch," to no one.

That's why I'm smarter than the average bear and enlisted the presence of my buddy Welton to be with me to view this video for the first time. If what I imagined about me being out there all alone was true, at least I'd have a lap to jump into. My grandma was long gone.

The video turned out perfectly. Max is there and he is definitely bringing the heat, not in the nineties any longer, but somewhere in the eighties. That's still some serious heat for someone in their middle 60s.

Sadly, this was the last time I was to see my friend Max for a while. In 1995, I became a fulltime student at North Carolina State University: Home of the Wolfpack!

Go Pack! Oops. Sorry.

Max had lost some off his fastball, but he was still bringing some 64-year old smoke. These three photos were taken from the short video I took in 1994.

I wonder how many 100-mph fastballs have passed through this old tire.

Max told me he thought some guy was hiding out in the gazebo watching him. Made my skin crawl.

Chapter 17

Aт NCSU, I arranged my eighteen-hour semester load so I had classes all day (and into the evening) on Tuesdays and on Thursdays. I used the other three weekdays and the weekends to sub as a teacher at various schools in Wake County and study diligently for all my courses. Mostly I just sat around and tried to figure out which end was up.

Every class I took had lots and lots of reading and lots and lots of writing about all the stuff I was reading. There were projects to do and papers due already almost before the semester began. At some point, I realized that much of it was just hoops set up for me and my classmates to jump through. For some of the assignments, there was no rhyme or reason for much of it. I believe a lot of it is done just to see who will jump through the hoops and who won't. Had I been a younger man, I might have told them exactly where to shove those hoops, one at a time.

Age has a way of quelling that knee-jerk, up-yours reaction to bullshit that sometimes leads to big trouble and heartache for the inexperienced youth. Yep. This age thing definitely has its strong points.

I can see it now. A potential employer rapidly skimming over my excellent grade transcripts, various honors, etc., and finally getting to the last page and the meat of the matter: SUCCESSFULLY JUMPED THROUGH ALL THE HOOPS.

"You're hired, Mr. White. We've been looking for someone like you. Welcome aboard!"

"Thank you. Thank you very much," I would say, in my best Elvis impersonation. "I could have been here sooner but I had to jump through all those bullshit hoops some idiot set up for me in college."

"You're fired! How the hell did you get in here? Take a hike!"

Oops.

Note to self: Keep in mind from this point on that you are no longer young.

Jameson and Taylor helped me tremendously during this period. Even at such young and tender ages, they realized I was doing something important and did their very best to play well together and give me quiet time to read and study. I made good grades because I wanted to do well, but more than anything in the world, I wanted my family to be proud of me.

Many times I thought about taking a few hours to go see how Max was doing, but just as many times I found reasons (or they found me) for not going. Schoolwork, honey-dos, coaching my son's not one, but two baseball teams, car trouble, truck trouble, and a job on the side all conspired to keep me busy and free from free time.

Time kept rolling and in early May '96 I was doing very well in most of my classes, but really struggling big time in the last math class I hoped I would ever have to take *in my life.* You want solid proof that the Lord works in mysterious ways? If my Sunday School teacher, Bob Martin, hadn't been the Dean of the School of Math at NCSU, I'd still be there now trying to get out of college. He put a word or ten in the ear of the grad student who was teaching that Mathematics of Finance class and I passed it by the breadth of a very fine frog hair.

I don't like to repeat myself but praise the Lord!

On another downside, I had also just made a 68 on a political science exam that morning. Did I mention that I hate politics? The only thing I hate worse is politicians, so why was I forced to endure such a class? I'll tell you what they told me: To make me a more well-rounded individual. To that I coughed rather loudly into my hand to disguise my proclamation of "Bullshit!" I still got a couple of laughs anyway.

More well-rounded, like, my ass.

My classes were over by 3:00 p.m. on Tuesdays this particular semester. Since my wife worked in Raleigh, and my kids attended school in Raleigh, and I also attended school in Raleigh, it only made sense for us to all ride together, with me being the cab driver on that day. I'd drop them all off in the morning and pick them up by four o'clock that afternoon.

This one particular afternoon, my professor decided to extend my final class by about twenty minutes. Oh, boy. If I take the time to find a telephone to call my wife and my kids' school, I'll be another ten minutes late. The decision, another bad one, was made – to hell with calling. When class was finally over, I literally stomped that mile and a half to my parking space as fast and hard as I could. I mumbled some real vile stuff about that professor all the way from Poe Hall to the other side of the Doak Field parking lot.

I was out of shape at the time, so that explained my being out of breath when I finally got there. I then leaped, well, fell into my car and headed out of the gravel parking lot toward the street when a damn *real* cab pulled right in front of me and stopped, blocking the only exit out of the lot.

Snap. (That was something in my head.)

"I don't have time to kill somebody right now," I thought. *"I got to go! Get outta my damn way!"*

Actually, I wasn't thinking those words. I was experiencing pure, unadulterated road rage and I was screaming them very loudly, drowning out the Doobie Brothers singing *Rockin' Down the Highway* blaring wide open on my radio.

I glanced at the clock above the radio and saw that I was still roughly twenty minutes late. My wife and my kids are going to be pissed. I looked up and the cab was still there, yellow as a big fat canary, and ruining my life.

I took both hands off the wheel and was about to blast a double-handed, sustained honk point blank into the side of that sucker when the back door slowly opened. I froze. I stared, transfixed, as Max Mangum got out of the cab, handed the driver some money, and then walked across the end of street to Doak Field where NC State's baseball team was practicing.

I guess he was just trying to find some loggerhead to have a fun game of catch. Like here, catch this if you can.

Now this is just uncanny. How much stuff had to jive together for this to happen? How about a little instant karma with your horoscope? It was then I realized that nothing we do is by chance. Only the guiding hand of God can pull off something like this, and He don't do much astrology.

I watched Max approach the fence that surrounded Doak Field. He just stood there, on the outside looking in, watching the young men of NC State's baseball team readying themselves for the day's practice. There were lots of people milling around in the entrance area, but no one even noticed him standing there. Maybe he really is a phantom. Mentally, though, I chalked it up to 'close encounters of the 7th kind' because that was about the seventh time our paths had crossed.

Since I was in a great big hurry, as always, I didn't even have time to stop for a minute and speak to Max. *"There won't be any rose-smelling today,"* I thought. After a moment or two of shock, I closed my mouth, slapped myself back to my senses, and drove away at the speed limit to retrieve my family. I was already late; no need to rush now.

I picked up the kids first and then Pam, and yes, they were ticked off a little bit, but I hoped that telling them about seeing Max at Doak Field would take a little of the edge off the situation.

"You'll never guess who I saw as I was coming out of the parking lot when I left school," I said with some strained excitement.

"Why are you so late?" Pam asked in her two-octave higher-than-normal voice that was generally a dead give-away that my ass was in hot water whether I wanted a bath or not.

"I saw Max," I said, answering my own question and delaying the answer to hers. "You know, the guy I wrote the story about." I chanced a glance to the right and met Pam's glare – whoa! – and immediately wished I hadn't.

Talk about angry eyes. If she was any kind of shot at all, I would have been DOA at Wake Medical Center.

"Is that why you're late?" Similar tone, maybe half an octave higher. *Oh, shit.*

"No," I said, "I was late because the professor held us for twenty minutes to finish a lesson." I explained about the taxi blocking me in and Max emerging from it.

Not impressed. "You could have called." Previous octave level maintained.

I pulled out into traffic on Jones Street and said, "Yeah, but I would have been ten minutes later if I'd tried to find a telephone. Why are you mad?"

"I'm not mad," Pam said, just one octave away from cracking the windshield.

"Good," I said. "Let's go to Char-Grill!"

Jameson and Taylor had been silent during our 'discussion' but came to life at the mention of the best burger joint in Raleigh, not to mention best one on the planet. Their excitement drowned out the silence raging in the front seat.

Nuclear meltdown averted, at least temporarily.

I wouldn't dare disturb the sound of that silence.

It wasn't that bad, of course. I'm just picking at Pam. Some people say I'm worse than Jim Carrey when it comes to being overly dramatic.

Crossing paths with Max Mangum again so unexpectedly, though, did add another little chapter to a story that appeared to have no end.

Chapter 18

I HAVE A LOT OF SPECIAL MOMENTS and memories from my two years at NCSU and my first three years of teaching. At first I thought none of these events had anything to do with Max, but in essence, all of them do. If it had not been for our chance encounter in 1991, I would never have been at NCSU, or teaching, or coaching, or writing this story.

After meeting with my advisor one morning, I'd registered for classes for what was supposed to be my next to last semester. Later, too late, actually, I discovered that we had neglected to sign me up for a social studies methods class that I *had* to have that was only offered in that particular semester and not the next one. This is just another one of those items that go into my extensive file of items called This Shit Can Only Happen To Allen.

There we go. Let's put a little red tab on this one.

Oh, my. This was not going to go over well with my loving wife and CFO of our little White House. I'd been out of a steady job for more than three years, and no matter what promises we'd made and financial sacrifices we'd endured, the not-having-any-money shit was already tearing the blades off the fan and getting old quickly. Patience was hard to find.

And now, at the worst of times, I find out that I've got to go an entire semester extra just because we'd failed to sign up for the correct course? I say 'we' but ultimately, it had to be my fault. I'm a damn grown man. I was not going blame this situation on someone else, even though I really wanted to. When I asked myself how could I have been so stupid, I reminded myself of my extensive experience in that particular field.

I had to speak with my advisor again before I told Pam about this calamity. Surely, my advisor, Dr. Carol Pope, would help me out.

"Hey, Dr. Pope!" I said, busting up into her office and taking a seat across from her desk. "Would you mind calling my wife and telling her what happened?" I asked. "Pam's going to have at the very least two running hissy fits, with one of which possibly developing into a full-blown conniption. I want her to know that it wasn't all my fault."

My advisor took a sip of her coffee and said, "No, I'm sure there's some sort of by-law in the college handbook forbidding me to do that, Allen. But think of it this way: Don't worry. It's just one more semester. One semester, no problem."

"One more semester, huh?"

"Right. Six months. And then you graduate."

"You're sure?"

"Absolutely."

"OK," I said. I feigned thinking for a few seconds which is kind of second nature to me and said, "OK. Here's how we'll work this." I have no earthly idea why I decided to joke around with Dr. Pope at this particular time. Death wish? I said, "You take my salary for that six months and I'll take yours."

"Uh, what?"

"Yeah. You take my salary, which is nothing, but just for that six months and I'll take yours, and I don't even know what your salary is."

"I-I don't think that's possible, I-

"Don't worry. It's just for six months. One semester. No problem, right? One semester and then I graduate."

I hope she knew I was kidding.

Just to be sure, I laughed and told her I was kidding about the salary thing, but I was dead serious about her calling Pam. It was only then that she removed her foot from the panic button on the floor and released her grip on the 9mm in her purse. I'm kidding again.

But I did pass two security guys coming in on my way out.

Just kidding there, guys. Jeez.

During my student teaching in my final semester, I was offered a job with the Humanities Department at NCSU, where the new social studies textbooks for North Carolina were being developed. Could this possibly be compensation for my lost six months? Who knows? Who cares? Not me. It may not have been payback, but it was a pay*check*.

Thanks! I really needed that.

I *am* kind of creative sometimes and word got around, I guess. First, they told me to just read through the photocopied pages of the 6th grade textbook – nothing else. Now that was some easy money because reading was about all I'd been doing for the previous four years and I was getting fairly good at it. After that read-through, I was instructed to go back, reread it, and come up with some journaling ideas and maybe some bulletin board ideas.

They were impressed that I'd found and noted about fifty typos and other little mistakes, since it had already been proofread by some professional proofreaders. In a caption under a picture of Istanbul, Turkey, someone had identified the Bosporus Strait as the Dnieper River. The Dnieper is a long river, but it's not that long, unless it stays intact flowing southward through the Black Sea and becomes the Bosporus Strait.

I joined the textbook project too late to get my name in the front of the actual textbook with all the others who'd worked on it. Drats! But my name was included in the teacher resource handbook. Finally. My fifteen minutes of fame!

And they spelled my name wrong: Alan.

They got it right on the checks, though.

I graduated from NCSU in December of 1996 with a Bachelor of Science degree in Middle School Education and the right to teach Language Arts (English) and Social Studies in grades 6 through 9. Completely out of character for me, I had made the dean's list a couple of times, graduated with honors, and also received the Charles W. Harper, Jr. award for Outstanding Future Educator at the graduation ceremony. Teaching and coaching became my new profession in January of 1997.

I had come a long way in the last five years and I realized I owed much of that success to a man who lives in a different world. Max's world is one that I can't adequately describe and few can even understand. Everything happens for a reason, though, and I believe that our paths had crossed so I could write his story, even though bits and pieces of my own little life are thrown in there for good measure and logistical purposes. Ok. And for filler, too.

Meeting Max had directly led me become the teacher and coach I think I was always meant to be. I lost track of how many hoops I'd had to jump through within the past few years, and now that I had graduated college, I still wasn't finished jumping through hoops.

I'm going to pass on elaborating on what a freaking money-taking scam I know the Praxis tests are. These are tests that a person must pass before the state can issue you a license to teach. This sumbitch proved to be the biggest hoop of all for me. I will be simple in my explanation of why the Praxis tests almost drove me to drive to Princeton, New Jersey and go postal on bunch of useless, unsuspecting crooks and thieves.

At NCSU, I was taught how to teach language arts and social studies to *middle school students* and, if necessary, to *ninth grade students*. The Praxis test I had to pass was geared toward high school. The biggest part of the test, and most subjective, was to outline a 6-week course of study for an 11th grade class. Twice I failed the test, first by 2 points and the second time by 1. I finally passed it on the third try, but that's not the point. The point is that something so subjective (influenced by personal feeling, tastes, and opinions) can determine whether someone is qualified to teach or not. I wanted to take my Outstanding Future Educator Award to Princeton and shove it up– well, I can't tell you what I wanted to do with it. Perhaps you can figure it out from the context clues.

Sorry. I could go on about this, but like my wit, it's pointless. Let's get back on track.

The first job I landed was indeed in January of 1997, an interim position for a teacher out on maternity leave. My first principal, John Wall of Zebulon Middle School, read and enjoyed my most current rendition of "Phantom of the Bullpen" and gave me permission to share it with my seventh graders. This one was a much tamer version of the story and contained very little personal information about me. I used some milder words here and there, changed this concept a little, and the story became suitable for kids in middle school.

Aside from the "Phantom of the Bullpen" being a good story, I began to use it every spring with my students in Language Arts. I taught reading, spelling, new vocabulary words, revising, editing, foreshadowing, oxymorons, similes, alliteration, hyperbole, perseverance, ask the author, and respect all people and life, among other things.

The students really seemed to enjoy the story and they loved watching the few minutes of video I have of Max. In addition, we watched the movie "Field of Dreams" and had popcorn and sodas as a culminating event. Did I know how to spoil children or what?

Near the end of the movie, when Costner, his voice cracking with emotion, asks his dead dad, "Wanna have a catch?" I can't help but sigh and shed a tear because I never got to have a game of catch with my dad. Never met him. Woe is me. Not really. But it does generate that one little lonesome tear in the corner of my eye.

Every. Single. Time.

"Mr. White's crying!" someone always yells.

But I'm ready. "No, I'm not. I got some salt from the popcorn in my eyes," I say in mock indignation.

"Sure you did," someone will say. "And salt makes your lower lip quiver, too, doesn't it, Mr. White?"

"No," I say meekly. "That's just a, uh, that's just a nervous tic."

During the 1997-98 school year, my first full year of teaching, I taught at Wake Forest—Rolesville Middle School. Sure enough, one of my students discovered that he was a distant relative of the "Phantom" and the students really connected with the story. They all wanted to hijack an activity bus (an idea which I seriously entertained for a few minutes), drive it to Max's house, and play some baseball. I could just see Max's reaction to a hundred screaming adolescents taking over his field.

No. I lied. I couldn't see that at all.

I ended up over-explaining why we couldn't go to Shade Stadium to spend a day with Max. The students had forgotten they'd even asked by the time I had paraphrased my reasoning for the third time. I swear, kids today have no attention span. Now isn't that a lovely butterfly? How 'bout them Yankees? I'm hungry. Look! A squirrel! Ok, who farted? Lunch! I gotta go to da baffroom…

At the end of my second full year of teaching in May of 1999, one of my students at Bunn Middle School, Gabe Ingino, gave me a very nice present. The gift was the 1999—2000 Writer's Guide to Book Editors, Publishers, and Literary Agents. Gabe said I should have "Phantom of the Bullpen" published. I was flattered, to say the least, and it enabled me to secretly return a similar book I'd held hostage for a year from the Zebulon Public Library.

I've always dabbled in writing: poems, lyrics, short stories; but even more so in college. Dr. Mattern at Nash Community College told me to always save every essay and any other kind of writing assignment, because you never know when you may get an opportunity to use it again, or expand upon it for a longer, stronger piece.

Once again, the lady was full of good advice and I took it. I've written several short stories that I'd like to work on, expand, and finish, but I can't get serious about them until I complete this little story.

Inspired only by Gabe's gift, I sat down one day in June that year and wrote the first 100 pages of my debut novel. It's a real thriller about bioterrorism, born and raised in the sands of the Arabian Peninsula and the rugged mountains of Afghanistan and Pakistan and brought directly to a home near you. It has many twists and turns that will keep the reader turning the pages well into the night. It should debut in about fifty years; I'm still on page 101.

I was motivated to write purely by the thought of this gift, because I had yet to look inside it. But I knew that when I did happen to finish one of these writing projects that I've gotten myself involved with, I'll have somewhere to find an agent or a publisher.

Yeah, right.

I probably should say something about the time the video of Max went missing. It was during my third year of teaching and we'd just finished reading the story and answering all the comprehension questions and a few critical thinking responses. (Critical to me, at least.) My students were chomping at their bits to see the video of Max, but I couldn't find it. Like Max did when I first met him, it had disappeared. And like all good teachers, I had always located all the resources I needed before beginning a unit, except for this time. I knew I could find the tape among our hundred or so unlabeled videos at home anytime I wanted to.

Not this time. Remember my luck?

"I thought we was going to see the tape of the old man pitchin' today, Mr. White," exclaimed, uh, Dennis.

I'm sorry. I'm not even going to act like I remember the name of the kid who said that. I can still see his little Dennis the Menace-like face, but his real name escapes me.

"'We *were*, Dennis, not we *was*,'" I corrected. "The word 'we' is plural. And yes, I did, too," I said. "I think my son or my daughter hid it from me."

"I hid my dad's cigarettes one time," he said.

"Good for you!"

"Not really. He found 'em and said one of 'em was missing and whipped my ass, I mean, butt."

I gave him 'the look' and then asked, "Did you take one of the cigarettes?"

"Yes, sir."

"Did you smoke it?"

"Yes, sir," he said smiling. "But I didn't inhale." Smart kid. He might end up as president one day.

I looked at old home movies off and on for a year or more before I found the one I'd hidden it on. It is now clearly marked and is kept separate from the others. What is it with me, or with Max, or with Max and me, or any other combination thereof, and any kind of photographic equipment or material?

Maybe I have some kind of kinetic energy that zaps stuff, obscures stuff, and makes stuff disappear and I just don't know it. I've always tried *not* to notice how I regularly screw up electronic items. Radios, televisions, boom boxes. Nothing is safe around me. Now I'm scaring myself. But if it's true that some people can bend spoons with their minds, it's not out of the question that I can screw stuff up just by touching it. Do I really want to know what the deal is with cameras, film, videos, and Max?

No. No, I do not.

I'm not sure I could handle the truth, and the truth is, this strangeness that had been restricted to electronics, specifically cameras, was about to branch out into the most common and basic of materials on the planet: wood.

Chapter 19

Have I mentioned yet how I single-handedly lost the 2001 World Series for the New York Yankees? There's a good reason for that. If you thought I was a little bit crazy before now, this should seal the deal.

I think it was more Max's fault than mine, but I can't really prove his involvement beyond a reasonable doubt, so he has plausible deniability on his side. This little saga does, however, have his phantom fingerprints all over it, though.

I did my part and I accept the blame. But before you dismiss my claim, let me tell you exactly what happened and you tell me if I'm guilty or not. Please allow me to paint some background because there is no direct route to where we're going. It may take us a few minutes.

Get some chips and salsa, something to drink, and let's go. I'll take a Diet Pepsi, please. Thank you. Damn, this salsa is *good*!

In late October of 1998 I was coaching Jameson's fall rec league team and a 14-and under travel team comprised of the best talent I could pull from the Zebulon, Bunn, and Wendell area rec leagues. I don't enjoy comparing and contrasting, but sometimes it's a necessary evil. On a Little League rec league team (8 to 12-year old), you can have a great time playing baseball, but sometimes there are kids out there who don't want to be out there. This creates a dangerous situation and it has always concerned me.

I don't mean to be harsh, but when a screaming line drive misses a kid's head in right field by mere inches and he has no idea what all the excitement is about because he was trying to catch a grasshopper with his glove, you may have a problem. As in, who gets the blame if a kid gets hit in the face by a screaming line drive?

I don't care who gets the blame; I don't want it to happen! All I'm saying is that there were a few kids out there on the rec teams who didn't want to be there and, for that reason, they shouldn't have been there. Just because a parent wants their child to experience something doesn't make it right.

Who wants to experience plastic surgery or a fractured skull? I'm thinking nobody. Thank goodness most of those kids found other interests by age fourteen.

The baseball field can be a very dangerous place if you're not paying very close attention to everything that's going on at all times. And this strong caveat is from me, the guy who suffered a fractured jaw back in 1996 from a foul tip because he was standing inside the backstop, just off to the right behind the catcher, trying to see why this particular batter was having trouble making contact with the ball. *I* certainly didn't have any trouble making contact with the ball.

Can you say 'dumbass,' boys and girls? Sure you can.

Working with the travel team was just a little less stressful, if you get my drift. All those guys *wanted* to be on the field and acted accordingly. They were focused. I'm not saying they didn't try to get by with some innocent horseplay every now and then – they're still just kids – but the stink-eye usually put an end to it. If it didn't, ten minutes of sprinting foul pole to foul pole sure did.

One day, near the end of a great practice at the Community Park in Zebulon with the travel team, a storm sneaked up on us and we had to scramble quickly to get off the field. We gathered up our gloves, bats, balls, donuts, coolers, empty cups, Gatorade bottles, and other assorted equipment and detritus and got the hell out of Dodge, er, Zebulon. There's always tomorrow.

Unless you get lit up by that one stray bolt of lightning.

When Jameson and I got home, we still had an hour or so before dark. We lived about five miles from Zebulon and the storm cell hadn't made it to our neck of the subdivision yet, so we decided to, uh, have a c-catch.

Jameson grabbed his glove and a baseball from the car, but when I grabbed for my glove, I came up empty. After searching the car frantically for about ten minutes, I determined that my glove must still be in its place in the corner of the dugout at the Community Park field in Z-town.

I'llberightback. Whoosh!

The rain was letting up as I turned into the entrance to the park. Immediately, I was taken aback at the sight of a taxi pulling out as I was pulling in. There is no taxi service in little old Zebulon, but there was one in service that evening. Since this taxi was leaving a ballfield, I instantly thought of Max and our brief encounter a few years back at the Doak Field parking lot on the campus at NC State.

I didn't get a great look at the passenger in the backseat of the taxi, but I got a good enough look to see that this person certainly *could have been* Max Mangum. But through a pair of rain streaked and fogged up windows, it could have just as easily been Will Geer or Cliff Johnson. It was too close to call.

I drove my car around the complex to the backside of W.G. Griswold Field and got out. The rain had fizzled to a pitiful drizzle, so I took my time getting to the dugout. Dodging mudpuddles to get there, the first thing I noticed was that my glove was not where it was supposed to be, nor was it anywhere else in the dugout. Shit! I searched under the bench and behind the bench. I searched the rafters in the roof above the bench. No glove. I loved that glove! I wanted to cry. I'd had it for at least twenty years. That glove had never made an error and it fit me like a, well, like a damn glove!

Then I saw it.

Not my glove. Standing up in the back corner of the dugout against the metal pole where my glove usually is, was a wooden baseball bat.

What? How did I not see that! It was the first place I looked for my glove*! Welp, there goes my Mr. Observant Award for this year,* I thought.

None of my players use a wooden bat! They all had nice, new aluminum jobs, one of which costs more than every glove and bat that I'd ever owned combined. I couldn't swear to the fact that this bat hadn't been in the dugout during our practice because I don't hang out in there. But I can swear to the fact that I'd never seen the damn thing before.

Where did the bat come from? Did someone make a trade without consulting me first? Did Max do it? *What are you doing to me now, Max?* I figured that I'd had about all the life-changing events that I could stand for one lifetime, so Max probably didn't have anything to do with the bat. But there again, I've been bitten in the ass by a 'probably' or ten over the years. This was difficult to shrug off.

It's probably nothing though.

I picked up the weapon of mass destruction for a closer look. Damn, what a heavy bat. I'd been accustomed to picking up just any one of the players' sticks when I hit infield and outfield to prove to them that the bat didn't matter all that much when it came to hitting. It's all about hand/eye coordination, concentration, and *knowing* that you can hit. It's no minor accomplishment to alternate between hitting ground balls and then pop flies using a little round ball and a big round bat. Try it sometime and get back with me.

The bat was heavy; no doubt about that. It was your basic 'flame tempered' Louisville Slugger made by Hillerich & Bradsby at their factory in Louisville, Kentucky. This was a very nice baseball bat. Then I saw the autograph out there on the business end: Joe Torre. The 'JT4' was etched into the bottom of the knob. In his playing days, Torre was a catcher with the Braves, Cardinals, and Mets. At this minute, though, Joe was the current manager of my New York Yankees. I kind of shouted, "Yes!" and pumped my fist in the air and yes, I was all alone in a park in a misty rain near dark. Big deal. No one saw me.

Back at home that evening, I called Greg Johnson who was now the Director of the ZPRD and told him about my bad luck/good luck that evening. The first thing I did was put out an APB and a BOLO on my glove. Then I told Greg that if anyone claimed they had lost a wooden Joe Torre autographed baseball bat to tell them he hadn't heard a thing about it. Not really. I told him that I had it if anyone came looking. Dammit. Gonna be hard to take a bat away from the guy holding it, though. Just making an observation. I stood the bat up in the corner of my garage and didn't even bother to look at it again.

For almost three years.

And then, the world changed.

I was teaching 7th grade at Bunn Middle School on September 11, 2001. On the big television hanging from brackets on the wall of our classroom, my students and I watched live as the second plane hit the second tower. I walked to the front of the room and hesitated. Reluctantly, I wrote the name 'Osama bin Laden' in big red letters on the white tile board. I said, "This is the guy who's going to get nailed for doing this."

I'd learned all I could about bin Laden in 1999 while doing a little research for that novel I was working on but still haven't finished. He was responsible (or so I read) for the simultaneous embassy bombings in two African capitals in 1998. Even so, I had my doubts that a bunch of guys 6,800 miles away, sitting around in some caves in the Hindu Kush mountain range in Afghanistan wiping their asses with pebbles, could have pulled off something so sophisticated, so synchronized, and so precisely here in the US of A.

There has to be a fly or two in the ointment somewhere, I thought.

Still, I was shaken. To the core. My wife's brother, Wayne Fowler, was a pilot for Delta Airlines and he flew to Europe out of New York two or three times every week. My daughter Taylor and I had just returned from visiting Wayne and his wife Tracy in Brooklyn a little more than two weeks earlier. We had walked all over Manhattan and we'd seen those towers from street level. I was looking forward to seeing them again.

And now this none-of-my-business world-stage shit just got personal.

A little later I told my students that what they had just witnessed was going to change the world – the whole world. I also let them know that things were never going to be the same again. Did I know these things for sure? How could I tell these young people such things? Was I trying to scare them? *I don't know* is the answer to all three questions. Deep down, I just wanted to be wrong.

But I wasn't.

My students were excited, but they didn't get it. They were just 7th graders. Maybe one or two got it; but not the rest.

You want proof?

The next morning and all day long through all my classes, all the kids were very upset. Why? One reason. Because none of the television shows they normally watched were on the previous night.

That was the first sign right there.

"Why were your shows not on?" I asked, knowing that all one hundred fifty-seven channels at my house had been reporting on the terrorist attack since 9am the morning before. The vast majority of the kids replied that it had something to do with "that bombing thing in New York yesterday."

'That bombing thing.'

I rest my case.

This catastrophic event also made me wonder how Max was doing and what he thought about this world-changing development. I certainly didn't know for sure, but I doubt that he even gave it a second thought as he continued to chalk up the K's and mow down batters at Shade Stadium. I wish I could have paid him a visit, but I was too busy running around like a head with my chicken cut off under the pretense of protecting my family. Soon, Max. Very soon. And I'm coming with a brand new baseball and it's got your name on it.

Other things, not nearly as important, changed, too. Like the major league baseball season. All the games were postponed until September 18 while things got straightened out and secured. The playoffs were pushed back for a week, also. For an entire week, air traffic was halted nationwide. Well, not exactly nationwide. There were a bunch of bin Ladens who were allowed to fly from Florida back home to Saudi Arabia on 9/12.

Fly? Ointment?

Anyway, along about the middle of October, the Yankees were taking it on the chin from the A's, down 0-2 in the American League Division Series. *It's a best of five series, guys. Come on!* I silently pleaded.

I was at home watching the Game 3 playing out in Oakland. No score at the end of three innings, so I went out to the garage to smoke yet another cigarette. Yes, I smoke. Sue me. At least I don't smoke in the house. As I was walking around the garage looking at the same old shit I look at every time I go out there to smoke, my eyes just happened to fall upon the wooden baseball bat I'd found a few years earlier. I don't think anyone had touched it since I put it there; I knew I hadn't.

My truck and Pam's car were in the driveway for some odd reason, so I picked up the big bopper and took a couple of vicious cuts, just for fun. That not-so-swift move made me hurt like hell all over. Wrists, arms, shoulders, legs, back, and neck, but it felt good, too. Real good.

About that time I realized the Yankees were probably already batting, so I went back inside, bringing along my newfound wooden friend. On the way inside, I put the handle of the bat between my thighs and pulled it through, wiping off three years of dust on my shorts. Can't bring a dusty thing like that into the house! I plopped down on the couch got back into the game.

My wife and kids were asleep by then and I had the whole living room to myself, as long as I didn't make any noise.

As I sat on the edge of the couch in front of the television, I was gripping the bat like I was in the batter's box and I'd either start my swing if I thought the pitch was good enough to hit or release my grip and let it go if it wasn't. I don't remember who the batters were, but we managed to score a run in the top of the 4th for a 1-0 lead. When the A's came to bat, I set my heavy little buddy over to the side, cheesed up my fingers with Dorito dust, and prayed for outs. And got 'em. That lone run held up for the 1-0 win.

There may have been one fleeting thought about the bat being magic or whatever and me holding it during that half an inning helped the Yankees stay alive in the division series, but I let it go. I am not superstitious or any of that stuff, you know that, but I do like to think about the wild side occasionally, not that I'd ever take a walk on it or anything.

Again I wondered if it had been Max that day in the taxi when I lost my glove and found that bat. Was I in possession of a magic bat? Probably not. It would be much more likely if I got a job driving the Who's Magic Bus.

It wasn't something I did subconsciously, but without really thinking too hard about it, I was holding Mr. Bat when the fourth game of the series started. It took a couple of innings for us (the bat and me) to get the fire stoked, but when we did, we unleashed a serious ass-whooping on the Oakland A's in their own house. Power down, brother bat! Save some of that for the next game. By the time I got the bat back under control, the Yanks had won 9-2, pounding out 11 hits. And I stuck with my little obsession of putting the bat down when the bad guys were hitting.

I absolutely refused to actually believe it was the bat or me or even Max helping the Yankees, but it sure did look that way on the surface. Under the surface, though, lies reality and reality says that shit just ain't possible. Still, it was lot of fun to play harmless mind games, and with my family sleepy-dreaming all cozy and warm in their beds, no one was watching me as I was now taking full cuts at the strikes in my living room.

Is there a better recipe for disaster?

At this point, I was purposely not even looking at the bat when Oakland was hitting, much less touching it, and taking my cuts when New York was at bat. I think 'purposely' means that I was 'in with both feet' and totally committed to this thing, or probably should be committed somewhere. To prove to myself I wasn't obsessed with this nonsense, when the Yankees came to bat at home in the bottom of the 1st inning in game five, already down 1-0, I did not touch the bat. And we didn't score.

Shit. New plan!

When the Yanks came to bat in the bottom of the 2nd, after the A's scored yet another run in their half, you best believe I was swinging the big stick. Boom. And just like that it was 2-2. What in the world is going on here? I thought, *Max, if you have anything to do with this, I am not amused. Dazed and confused maybe, but not amused.*

Why can't I just be normal like everyone else? Strike that from the record, please. Why can't I just be normal like a few people I've heard of but never met?

It's a little too late to make a long story short, but Mr. Bat got us three more runs in that ALDS clincher and the Yankees won 5-3. In the American League Championship Series, it just got better and weirder. I put the bat down when the Mariners were hitting and I picked it up when the Yankees were at bat. The Yankees won the series 4-1 and the game they lost? Game 3? I missed that one because I was out of town.

Someone else will have to kindly tell me what the deal is because I was clearly not thinking clearing at that time. Or now, apparently.

Believe me, it's taking a lot of nerve for me to come clean about the bat, but here it is for you perusal. I wish I *could* make up shit like this.

In order to clear my mind, I decided to leave the bat in the garage during the World Series and get over it, whatever *it* was. I just needed to sit down and watch the ballgames and enjoy myself and stop practicing voodoo without a proper license before I hurt myself or somebody else. I had avoided getting zapped into a turd so far, so why tempt fate?

Because it's there. That's why.

What in the hell is wrong with me? Why am I obsessing over a baseball bat? Those are not the only questions I was asking myself. Did Max take a damn taxi to Zebulon, steal my glove, and leave me a magic bat in its place? The only problem with questions is that sometime you don't get any answers. And sometimes when you get the answers, you don't want them. All I was getting was a bunch of static.

Sticking to my guns and my resolve, the bat stayed in the corner of the garage as the 2001 World Series began in Arizona. The Diamondbacks beat the Yankees badly in the first game and easily in the second game.

I thought, *Well, that's about enough of this shit.*

I broke out Mr. Bat and we helped the Yankees win the next three games in New York to garner a 3-2 lead in the Series.

Take that! You filthy reptiles.

The Series went back to Arizona for the sixth game and try as we might, Mr. Bat and I just could not overcome the dominating pitching performance by Randy Johnson. He cuffed the Yankees and he cuffed me right there in my own damn living room. Big Unit, my ass!

Do you know what that monster did one time? With his fastball, he killed an innocent bird that just happened to fly between the mound and the plate while he was pitching! What a mean, mean man. Hollow bones and feathers are no match for baseball moving at 100+ miles per hour.

And neither were the Yanks that game.

I never mentioned to anyone – friend, foe, or family – about Mr. Bat and what was going on at my house during the 2001 playoffs and World Series. Never. Until now. Most folks already suspected I was a nut and the rest knew I was. The video of Max proved to some of them that he was for real and I was not totally crazy when it came to him, but this shit? This shit, if it got out, could really and truly get me committed.

I wonder what the statute of limitations is for temporary insanity?

If I'd said *any*thing to *any*one about Max giving me a magic bat that was helping the Yankees make comeback after comeback in the playoffs and the World Series? Shh. Look! Men in white coats with a really long-sleeved jacket with my name on it. Shh. Listen. Hear that? *They're coming to take me away ha ha hee hee.* No proof exists, but I know how to keep my mouth shut when my freedom is on the line.

World Series. Game 7. Is that a stage, or what?

Since Mr. Bat was ineffective the last game against Randy Johnson, I reluctantly decided it was probably all just coincidental anyway. I vowed to leave him leaning against the couch and only use him in case of an extreme emergency.

Five and a half innings of scoreless baseball can seem like a lifetime and there was no score in this one until the Diamondbacks tallied a run in the bottom of the 6th. It didn't take me long to recognize this situation for exactly what it was.

EXTREME EMERGENCY!

I picked up Mr. Bat and we tied the score in the top of the 7th. I put Mr. Bat back in his resting place while the Diamondbacks were shut down and out in the bottom of the inning. I snatched Mr. Bat from his moorings at the end of the couch and we produced another run for the Yanks in the top of the 8th, giving us a 2-1 lead. Mr. Bat's ass went right back to the couch where he belonged while Mariano Rivera came in and struck out the side and the D'Backs went down in the bottom of the 8th.

I didn't think we'd need an insurance run in the 9th because I was sure that Rivera was going to get the 2-inning save for the Yanks' third come-from-behind win in the playoffs. I mean, it's Mo, man. Turn out the lights; this party is o. v. e. r.

I may not have thought we *needed* any insurance, but I sure as hell *wanted* some! Employing the services of Mr. Bat in the top of the 9th just to be on the safe side, I put my death grip on the handle and tried to make splinters out of that Louisville Slugger. It was all for naught, though. We mustered absolutely zero mojo for the Yanks, not ever a baserunner, much less an insurance run.

But hey! We didn't need no stinking insurance run. Mo was coming back out in the bottom of the 9th to mow them scaley-hided suckers down.

I'm sorry. There is no way that I'm going to relive that train wreck that was the bottom of the 9th inning of the 2001 World Series by writing a blow-by-blow account about what happened and how it happened. One crazy damn thing after another happened, that's what happened, and none of it should have happened.

A quick summary should suffice: Baserunners, errors, a couple of hits, and it's tied at 2-2. Then, with the bases juiced, Joe Torre himself engineers a brain-fart shift that, in my humble opinion, should never have happened. The shift took Derek Jeter away from the exact spot where Luis Gonzalez reached out and dumped a dying-quail blooper on the next pitch to score Jay Bell from third to win the World Series for Arizona. I was crushed. Devastated. We were so very close.

And then I saw it.

Still in my hands and still in a death grip that would make a pair of Vise-Grip plyers jealous, was Mr. Bat. Without realizing it, I'd been holding Mr. Bat while the Diamondbacks – the opposing team, the enemy, the bad guys – were hitting! The biggest frigging no-no of all. I couldn't believe what I'd done! It scares me now to think just how close I came to slinging Mr. Bat through of one of my wife's lovely floor-to-9-foot-ceiling living room windows. That would have caused quite a stir in the southern White House and I'm not talking about the night air blowing through.

In a flash, I saw myself flying to New York and getting there about the same time the Yankees would be getting back the next day. The one fellow I was looking for would be easy to spot. He's got a 5 o'clock shadow twenty minutes after he shaves in the morning and besides, he's a dead ringer for Fred Flintstone. Yaba daba doo! – Boom Boom! Out go the lights! As evil as it was to even imagine it, I was going to beat Joe Torre with a baseball bat bearing his very own signature.

How cool, I meant, how crazy would that have been?

It was at that moment that I realized the Yankees 1-run loss to the Diamondbacks in Game 7 of the 2001 World Series was not Joe Torre's fault; it was mine.

I had failed to do my part. I forgot to put down the bat while the snakes were hitting.

And that is how I single-handedly lost the 2001 World Series for the team I'd loved for forty years.

With or without Max's help, of course.

Chapter 20

I MADE SEVERAL ATTEMPTS to contact Max after the World Series in 2001. Twice when I called, his sister told me that Max was sick and she didn't think it would be a good idea for him to see me. What? Did she think that I was gonna drag him out of his sick bed and out into the yard to play catch? Come on, Mrs. Davis! Gimme a break here. I was thinking I could maybe prop him up on a few pillows and toss a couple of innings from the bedroom to the living room, but it wouldn't have gone any further than that. I'm not stupid.

Just kidding; I'm a kidder.

The third time I called, Mrs. Davis asked me very sweetly, "Would you consider saying a few words about Max at his funeral if he should pass away due to his current ailment?"

Whoa. Hold up, lady. Death has always freaked me out so I flatly refused and told her why.

"Look, I'm gonna die way before anybody else I care about dies and that's just the way it is so there is absolutely no need in discussing it any further because I couldn't possibly do that no way no how so can we change the subject please?" I said in a child-like flourish.

But later, after much thought, I decided that, if I happen to still be on this side of the dirt when Max passes away, I would be more than honored to share a few choice words with his family and friends. Saying something nice about Max Mangum at his funeral would be the least I could do for the man who, in a perfect world, probably would have had the Cy Young Award renamed after him.

I called Mrs. Davis on the last day of March in 2002 to inquire about Max and to inform her of my change of heart. She was happy that I had reconsidered and consented to speak at Max's funeral. And then we proceeded to go round and round again about how she felt the story about him might embarrass the family, and why I shouldn't have it published.

I told her as I always had, that I would respect her wishes, but she was really missing the point if she thought the story would be the least bit embarrassing for Max, or for her, or for her family in any way. In fact, I thought the story, when published, could lift Max and his family to superstar status overnight. I told her that I would let her read the finished product before I tried to get it published because I wanted her approval above all else.

At last, Mrs. Davis finally relented and verbally gave me permission to write the story about Max as I saw fit and to go ahead and have it published.

Oh, if it were only that easy.

She also gave me permission to visit her brother the following day although he was 'feeling poorly' when she saw him the previous day. Somehow she delivered the message to Max, and he was waiting for me, once again, on the first day of April.

By now, my little story of the "Phantom of the Bullpen" had come full circle. I stood there in Max's yard with a relatively new (but borrowed) glove on one hand and a brand new baseball in the other. As best I could figure, it was exactly ten years to the day since my first visit there.

Just another April Fool's Day.

Max was kicked back on the front porch swing smoking a big, fat Cuban cigar and nursing a Long Island Ice Tea in a tall glass. The glass was sweating. So was I.

He was wearing a misshapen, dusty old Yankees' hat, a way-too-short royal blue silk Lakers' jersey with Kobe's number 8 in gold, a lime-green Speedo, and a pair of jet black baseball shoes with metal spikes filed to sharp points and no socks.

I noticed he had thick ankles. On his right ankle was a tattoo of a tick. Or, it may have been a real tick. I wasn't there to check for ticks.

Ha. April Fool.

Actually, Max was resting in a lawn chair out in the backyard, so we didn't make a trip to Shade Stadium. He had been throwing to one of those nets on a stand with a canvas batter outlined in white against the blue background. I don't remember what they are called, obviously. I remember Mrs. Davis telling me a few years back that it had been a present from Mr. Phil Johnson of Johnson-Lambe Sporting Goods in Raleigh, again, not to be confused with *our* Phil Johnson, who pitches for the Zebulon Pirates.

We shook left hands and I asked Max, "Do you remember who I am?"

Max looked *at* me, then he looked *through* me, then he gazed off into the distance *beyond* me, and then looked quickly back *at* me. He said, "I know who you are if you are who you say you are." He turned his head and looked toward net guy and then back to me again.

I heard what he said but I couldn't come up with an honest answer, because in essence, he had offered an extremely deep response and I didn't fully grasp the significance of his words at the time. I just said, "Good. How have you been? I ain't seen you in nearly five years."

It took me a few more seconds but I finally got it. I'd forgotten that, to Max, I was and always would be, a scout for the Pittsburgh Pirates.

Max was quiet for a few seconds. A large black bird flew overhead and we watched it disappear over the rusty tin roof of his house. "A lot can happen in five years," Max said.

"You're telling me, brother," I said, flashing back on all that I'd endured to become a teacher and a coach, which is nothing when compared to what Max had endured during the past fifty years trying to become a major league pitcher.

There were many times while attending Nash Community College and North Carolina State University when I'd stayed up all night long on a reading assignment or writing a damn paper and thought I wasn't going to make it. Then I'd picture Max clinging desperately to the single vision of what he thought he should have been doing for the last half century: pitching in the major leagues.

I remain speechless about what kind of tenacity, energy, and faith that kind of focus must have required.

That was about all the small talk Max could stand and I was about to get all philosophical when he said, "I been throwin' a while this mornin' but I'll let you get another look. You still with the Pirates?" he asked.

"Max, I'm not with anybody anymore. I'm teaching seventh grade English this year and I coach our middle school baseball team," I confessed, bragged. "I haven't played baseball for several years."

He threw me only a handful of pitches. Max could hardly get the ball back to me and we were only about 40 feet apart. It was as though he had aged fifty years in less than ten. He still looked the same; just like Will Geer minus the gray moustache, but the man with the flaming fastball had, in fact, left the bullpen.

Between the second and third tosses, I asked Max, "Did you take a taxi to Zebulon a few years ago?" Max snagged the ball and stared me down.

A few seconds passed before he answered.

"I went to that field at that school where I pitched one day, but nobody was there!" he exclaimed. "That cab driver, he found another field, but it was rainin' and fixin' to get dark and it won't nobody there, neither."

So, it *was* Max that I saw that day. I think I knew it all along.

Max soft-tossed me another pitch and said, "I see you got yourself a new glove." He gave my borrowed mitt a nod and looked away.

I just smiled and shook my head and said, "Sure did." If he had asked me how I liked the bat he'd left for me, I can honestly say that I most assuredly would have, without hesitation, forethought, or shame, shit my pants right then and there. No hyperbole; no exaggeration. He didn't, though. He just sighed and glanced over at the canvas guy.

Either way, I wasn't going to say anything about the bat. There is no way in the world I was going to knowingly step right into the middle of Twilight Zone. I knew that I couldn't handle the truth, whatever it was. Plus, I didn't have a change of clothes with me.

Even if he had told me point blank that he'd taken my glove and exchanged it for a magical bat that would eventually bring down the mighty New York Yankees, what was I going to do about it? Ain't nobody gonna believe this shit anyway. It's kind of like the preacher who feigned sickness one Sunday morning to sneak off to a city some miles away just to play a round of golf by himself. St. Peter saw what the preacher was doing and ran to tell God and God said, "Watch this!" On #1, the preacher hit a massive 380-yard drive that bounced toward the green and rolled right into the cup for a hole-in-one. The same thing happened on #2 and on through #18. St. Peter asked, "Why did You let him have the best round of golf ever?" God simply said, "Who's he gonna tell?"

The fact that Max was still throwing the baseball around 90 miles per hour in his sixties was hard enough to swallow. Most people have a hard time wrapping their head around that little anomaly.

A magic bat? Forget about it.

I honestly don't care if anyone believes it or not. It could very well have been nothing more than a string of a hundred or so strange coincidences stretched out over the course of a few weeks that allowed the Yankees to score runs and kept their opponents from scoring during the playoffs. I'm sure it happens all the time. But that circumstantial evidence looms large from where I'm hiding, I meant standing.

Just saying.

I thought Max might need to conserve his energy, so I turned around and tried to sneak a strike by the canvas guy, but he was taking all the way and the ball kinda sailed behind his head anyway. *"Nice pitch, White,"* I thought. I retrieved the new baseball from the freshly cut grass and gave it to Max. Except for a small green stain across the Rawlings logo, it had plenty of white still on it.

He talked about the Astros for a few minutes, and then the Phillies. He said he was tired, and I said I had to get on back to the house, and that I'd come back someday soon.

It may have been my imagination, but he seemed a little put out because he couldn't throw the ball like he wanted to. Max hadn't lost command of his fastball; he'd lost command of his health. In the past, his body vibrated with enthusiasm for pitching, for baseball, for everything. Today he was struggling to stand, to walk. A distinct look of resignation etched his face and diminished his countenance to nearly nothing.

Looking up again, I saw the dissipating white vapor trail of a jet airliner pushing it softly, silently across the pale blue sky. *My God*, I thought, *there must be some way to make today last forever or at least just a little longer.*

I had hoped to see Max still throwing the rock at eighty or ninety-plus. I had hoped that somehow Max had stayed frozen in time the way I had pictured him for the past decade. And I hoped I had, too.

I wanted him to stay frozen in time because I felt as though I hadn't had ample time to get to know him well enough. We didn't get to talk enough or throw together enough. I would've loved to have taken him to a ballgame somewhere, but time kept marching on and I couldn't even find my boots.

My children had grown up so much in the past few years also. With me going to college, working odd jobs, studying all the time, and then trying to be the perfect teacher had robbed me of watching them grow. Sure, I was there, but usually my mind was spread out over a thousand acres. I felt so cheated, and the sad part was that I'd cheated myself.

"See ya, Max," I said, halfway hoping he might catch his second wind and suggest that we throw some more.

Max nodded once and disappeared inside his back door.

I went home.

I was also hoping for a better ending, but I think I used them all up at the end of some other chapters.

Good.

I didn't want this to be the end of the story anyway. Something else, however, was ending and hitting much closer to home.

Chapter 21

A LITTLE MORE THAN A YEAR after my visit with Max in 2002, Pam and I separated. We had been married for twenty years and two days. Separating was not an easy decision, but it was one that I had been struggling with internally on a daily basis for several years and more than likely, so was Pam. Something like that is not fair to anyone. The constant tension and too many heated discussions were just not conducive to a happy home.

Maybe splitting up is selfish but I believe that I did what I did for Pam and Jameson and Taylor, as much as for myself. It seemed that the harder Pam and I tried to get it right, the more it just kept going the other way. There was never any violence involved, but the pain was unbearable.

On June 15, 2003, I had reached my limit. I had to go because I knew in my head and in my heart that I couldn't take another minute of what we were going through. I knew for a fact that I could never and would never hurt Pam or my children or anyone else, for that matter. That left just me, and even with all my faults, quirks, idiosyncrasies, and bad habits, I kind of liked me.

My life had never been anything close to a picnic and there had been more than a few times when I felt that I was at the end of my rope, but I'd never seriously considered suicide. I always did what every man, woman, or child did who loves life no matter how deep the shit piles up: I tied a damn knot at the end of that rope and hung on tightly.

Suicide is never an option when you always believe that one day, someday, it's all going to be all right.

I needed to be close to my family even if my wife and I could no longer live together, so I rented a small house about five miles away. That way, I was able to continue to take Taylor, who was fourteen at the time, to school every morning until she got her driver's license when she turned sweet sixteen.

I must have unconsciously done things to provoke Pam to say things that hurt me deeply. I pray she knows that I would have never done anything to purposely hurt her. There were times during some of our heated 'discussions' that I'd retaliated with some low-blow barbs trying to hurt her verbally as I was being hurt, but I certainly didn't enjoy it. In the end, I left due to a bad-to-severe case of irreconcilable differences.

Pam and I were divorced one year after the separation.

Jameson had graduated from Bunn High School a few weeks before I changed my address. He had stopped playing baseball at fourteen because I had burned him out on the game. I had him swinging a big orange plastic bat and crushing homers across the yard and across the street when he was only two and playing t-ball at four. By the time he got fed up with baseball, he was playing recreation league and travel ball. At the tender age of fourteen, he already had ten years of experience in the game.

He had taken up golf when he was about twelve and learned the game over next few years. While in high school, Jameson started swinging the golf club more seriously and became a valuable member of first East Wake's and then Bunn High's golf teams. He moved in with me in October. I hate to think what may have happened to me if I'd been left alone during those first few months of separation.

There were many dark days and even darker nights.

Taylor came to stay every other weekend until she graduated from Bunn High three years later. During her junior year in high school, she won the state 2-A championship in the 100-yard breaststroke.

She had worked very hard to earn it, too. Every day since she was about 12, Taylor had an early-morning practice and an evening practice with her swim team in Raleigh, not to mention swim meets every other weekend. In between practices, she went to school in Zebulon (in Bunn for 8th grade and high school) and took care of her schoolwork. She had the drive and discipline I lacked at that age.

I like to think that she got her athletic ability from her dad, but she definitely got the intelligence and swimming from her mom. I have to wear water wings in the bathtub.

That's just between us, okay?

Taylor attended college at the University of North Carolina in Wilmington and came home often during her freshman year. After that, though, she made Wilmington her home.

Everybody loves their children, so there's no need for me to try and tell you how much I love mine. If I did that, this would be the longest book ever written and I'd still be writing.

I have time. though, if you do.

I never got the chance to play baseball again. Coaching and managing the middle school team was enough to keep me happy on that front. Thank God for cable and dish television. With DirecTV's MLB Extra Innings package, I was able to watch every Yankee game I desired until I had to give up television completely.

One word: commercials. I hate them and they drive me insane. Yes, I know it's a short ride, but I still don't want to go. When I watch a baseball game, I don't want someone trying to sell me the same car or truck fifteen times that I don't want and can't afford. And then here comes some idiot trying to convince me fifteen times that I need some kind of miracle medicine that will cure my heartburn but may also make my eyes bulge, cause my spleen to shrivel up and fall off, and leave my asshole bleeding. The trade-off hardly seems worth the trouble. I'm just not interested. Sorry.

More pizza over here! Thank you.

I do have a nice, short baseball story to relate. In August of the year I moved out, 2003, my old Pirate teammate and long-time friend Randy Pearce called me and asked if I'd mind throwing batting practice to his 14-year old all-star team from the Wendell recreation league. He thought they needed to get a look at a lefty for their upcoming state tournament. I usually pitched some BP to my middle school team every spring, so I readily agreed.

Now I'm not saying that Randy is one of those guys who never says what he means or means what he says, but I didn't pitch BP to his kids that day. What Randy did was divide his boys into two teams of seven players each, add a dad to each squad, and put me on the mound to pitch to both teams.

I was forty-eight at the time and I was pitching to the cream of the crop of fourteen year-olds from the Wendell area, not to mention that dad on each team. In my little mind, I saw that as about even. And it was.

I pitched seven innings (fourteen half-innings) of scoreless baseball that afternoon, walked nary a one, and even had a couple of strikeouts. I somehow managed to work out of three or four bases-loaded jams. The kids on both teams played great defense behind me and Randy and I were both very pleased.

One of the dads took advantage of my severely diminished fastball, though, and nearly tore my damn head off with a rip up the middle in the third inning, but that's ok. 'Nearly' is a magic word when it comes to the damage a batted baseball might have done. I mean, really. That line drive could have ricocheted off my head and hurt one of those kids! I was sore all over for about three weeks after that game.

A footnote for Randy's team: they won the North Carolina Dixie League championship about two weeks after getting that look at a lefty.

Chapter 22

And then, while I wasn't looking...

Five more years slipped by. Five more calendars used up their useful-ness and went into the trash. And five more baseball seasons were in the books.

Five years *is* a long time and I can't recall a single day of it that I didn't think about Max in some way, shape, or form. I was somewhere in the mid-dle of my summer vacation (from school, at home, not in Jamaica) in 2008 when I tried to contact Max again. I found the number for his sister, Mrs. Davis, and gave her a call, hoping that she was doing well and would still remember me.

Sometimes I think the scariest sound ever is that 3-note electrical tone followed by *"We're sorry, but the number you have dialed is no longer in ser-vice."* If you're calling someone fairly young it's no big deal. Young people move around. But when you're calling someone with some age on them, that noise is like a death knell.

And it was.

I did a little digging and found out that Doris had died in 2005, about a year after her husband Edwin had died. Death. I don't like it, but it's as much a part of life as, uh, well life itself.

The only thing I knew to do then was to go to Max's house and drop in uninvited. I parked my car in front of his house and went to the door and knocked. I can't really describe the deep and immense silence that engulfed me, so I won't even try, but it was deathly quiet out there that day.

I walked around back. Canvas guy was still out there, looking a little mildewed, but still begging for another pitch. I ignored his taunt and knocked

on the back door and called Max's name. I was making the only noises to be heard. No birds, no cars passing by, and no breeze. No nothing.

I walked back to my car and started my 20-minute drive home. The closest house to Max's place is about fifty yards away, and there was a guy standing in the front yard. I don't like surprising people, but my car didn't know that. The steering wheel veered to the right and my arms went with it. I parked in the guy's driveway and walked over to him and introduced myself.

I don't remember his name but he was a very nice fellow, about my size and build, just not as old and gray. I asked him about Max and I had to hear some things I really didn't want to hear. He told me that back in February, they had found Max asleep on his porch at about eight o'clock in the morning. The temperature was in the low 30's and he had nearly frozen to death. He was certain they had taken him to Dorothea Dix Hospital in Raleigh, but he had no idea if he was still there. The man also told me that he thought Max's niece was trying to watch out for and take care of Max, but "Old Max is kinda bullheaded sometimes and don't like nobody tellin' him what to do."

I left the gentleman my telephone number and asked him to call me if he found out anything else about Max. I waited a couple of days, but not knowing anything was killing me.

Sitting down in front of a most wonderful machine, I instructed my old Packard (Hewlett Packard) to find me some information on one Gaius Max Mangum. Of the many hits with various combinations of Max's name, only one proved fruitful, and I needed only one. There was a note posted in the Woodland Baptist Church bulletin (online) in the form of a prayer request from Suzanne Landis for her uncle, Max Mangum. Woodland Baptist is the church where Max's sister Doris worshipped. Finally, the odds were kind of in my favor, I had 'em but nowhere near as good as 5-1.

I called the number on the church's home page and spoke to the secretary. I intended to give her my number and then pray that Suzanne Landis would call me back, but the secretary gave me Suzanne's telephone number without even questioning me.

Suzanne Landis actually knew who I was so I didn't have to expla anything to her. She told me she had the copy of the story I'd given her moth long ago and the issue of <u>HardBall Magazine</u> that contained the first few pa

of my Phantom of the Bullpen story as well. I asked how Max was getting along and she told me he was doing ok, but he was more or less bedridden.

She said it was strange that I had called just now because she and a friend were going to visit Max the next day. She asked me if I wanted to meet them at the Brian Center, a long-term health and rehab hospital/nursing home in Wilson where Max now lived.

No, not really, I thought.

Too many scary movies and bad television shows have hospitals as their settings. I don't like going anywhere near hospitals; don't even like driving by them on the highway. Plus, I didn't want to see Max infirmed, but she didn't offer any other options because there were no other options.

I'd been to one too many hospitals and rest homes to visit friends and older family members, and no matter how good my intentions may have been, the places always depressed the hell out of me. I guess that pretty much nails down what my end days are going to look like, providing I'm that lucky. If I didn't meet Suzanne and her friend there the next day, I'd probably never see Max again.

It was time for me to really grow up. I had to overcome my selfishness and self-centeredness to do the right thing.

In a place like that, you see every kind of person with every kind of disorder that exists. It's not that I don't have compassion for the infirmed, I do, it's just that all I know how to do is feel sorry for them, and that helps no one. My plan was to stay focused on visiting with Max awhile and then politely get the hell out of there at the first available opportunity.

We met in the lobby at 11am. Suzanne Landis turned out to be every bit as charming as her mother had been. Suzanne told me she was a school teacher, like me, but had retired a few years back. She also told me that she was very happy that I was there to see Max. He didn't get a lot of visitors, she said, as she introduced me to her friend, Jane. We exited the lobby and took the elevator to the fourth floor. Suzanne and Jane went into Max's room first and I trailed behind, slowing down to stop in the doorway.

As she entered the room Suzanne asked, "Max, how are you feeling today?" He seemed mildly surprised and didn't respond right away. Max was

more interested in a recorded baseball game on the television hanging from the ceiling at the foot of his bed. Max turned and recognized his niece.

"Hey. What?"

"I asked how you are doing today?" she said.

"I'm ok, I guess," Max offered and looked back to the game.

Susanne said, "Max, do you remember my friend?"

Max looked back to Suzanne and then to her friend and said, "Yeah. Ya'll come in and sit down." Again, he looked back to the game.

Suzanne moved into the room a little further and touched Max's arm and said, "What about this man here, Max. Do you remember him?"

Max reluctantly turned away from the game, slowly turned his head past Suzanne, past her friend, and finally zeroed in on me. I was afraid he wouldn't have any idea who I was and maybe throw some kind of fit to get me removed or even locked up in some cell in the basement with shackles on the wall and a bloody stretch rack in the middle of the cold cement floor, beveled out so fluids could be washed down the drain.

Sorry. That imagination thing again.

I was ready to break all kinds of land speed records if the wrong thing happened. I certainly wouldn't want to, but I wouldn't be shy one bit about diving through a fourth floor window if I really had to. I can't swim, but I figured I could fly, just not very far. Flying wasn't the issue. It was that sudden stop at the end of the flight that was going to be the problem.

Sorry. TMI. Too much imagination.

Max sat up quickly on his bed, never taking his eyes from mine. I was ready to bolt.

"Hello, Max," I managed to squeak out, sounding very much like a rookie Girl Scout trying to sell her first box of samoas.

Max didn't say a word. He threw the covers back and stood up. Thank God he wasn't going commando. Still maintaining eye contact, he walked around his niece and her friend and grabbed my right wrist firmly with his left hand. Too late to bolt now. With his free right hand, he opened the drawer on his little nightstand, reached in and removed a purple Nerf baseball.

He pulled me out into the hall and led me to the window at the end. He released his grip on me and walked back about twenty paces. "You still scoutin' for them sorry-assed Pirates?" he asked.

Whew! I finally breathed; a big sigh of relief that stirred the curtains over the window fifty feet away at the *other* end of the hall. Suzanne and I had already decided that I should tell Max whatever I thought might make him feel better if he happened to ask me about anything related to baseball.

I laughed and said, "I sure am, Max."

"They finally gettin' around to givin' me my chance?"

"Yes, they are. I just need to make sure you still got the heater."

My mind drifted back to the first time we'd met at Durham Athletic Park. I fondly recalled the heater that had so thoroughly grabbed my attention. Max's fastball was better in 1991 at the age of 62 than the fastball I had in high school at the age of 18 in 1973. I wasn't expecting that same heater here today, but if he had knocked my ass out of that window with a blazing purple Nerf ball, it would have only been fitting. But I still wasn't looking forward to that sudden stop at the end.

There was a guy sitting in a wheelchair just outside his own room, about halfway between Max and me. Young guy, looked to be maybe thirty, thirty-five, no more than that. He had been laughing when Max led me to the window, and he was still laughing hard about something. I just wish I knew what it was.

Max winked and said, "Well, let's see what happens."

Max took his little windup, rested for a second or two, and tossed me a perfect strike where I was squatting there at the end of the hall. Because of the texture of a Nerf baseball, it came to me in super-slow motion, but I would have waited all day for it.

Wheelchair Guy must have thought this was hilarious because he hit another gear in his heartfelt laughter. I thought he might fall out of the chair until I saw the seatbelt. I didn't think Max could catch the ball, so I jogged it back to him and returned to the imaginary plate at the end of the hall.

Max's next pitch bounced off Wheelchair Guy's head and then ricocheted directly to me at the end of the hall.

"Strike two!" I shouted. Wheelchair Guy was laughing so hard now tears were rolling down both cheeks. I think I might have had one rolling down my cheek, too. I must have been happier than I thought.

Max wanted to throw one more pitch, but I could tell he was getting weaker. "Ok, Max. You got two strikes on him. Finish him off," I said and handed him the ball again. He sighed heavily, did his little windup, sighed heavily again, and delivered another perfect strike. Wheelchair Guy clapped his hands and continued to cackle. Suzanne Landis and her friend smiled brightly.

When we got back inside Max's room, he said, "Did I do all right?"

"You did fine, Max. I'm going to tell them to write you a contract as soon as I leave here." Max was settling in under his covers, but he still looked very excited.

"How much do you want?" I asked, shucking the scout role for the general manager position. "I bet they'll give you any amount from here to Rocky Mount!" I said, trying to be funny.

Max didn't find it funny at all.

"What? Money?" he asked, and if I didn't know better, I'd say he asked the question incredulously.

"Yeah. How much do you want?"

Max looked at the game on television and then back to me. "I don't need your money. I told you that before," he said. "I just need to play some ball."

Some things change; some things don't.

In the movie "Field of Dream" Shoeless Joe Jackson admitted that he "would have played for meal money." I always thought that was a very strong statement, one of the strongest that I'd ever heard.

Max would have *paid* to pitch in the major leagues just to play some ball. That's a fairly strong string of words, too.

Max's lunch arrived a few minutes later and we said our goodbyes to Max and left. In the parking lot, I thanked Suzanne for allowing me the honor of visiting her uncle. I drove home on autopilot. I must have arrived safely or I wouldn't be writing this.

I couldn't have asked for, dreamed up, or fabricated a better ending. But what did Yogi say? It ain't over 'til it's over.

And sometimes, it still ain't over.

And it ain't over yet.

Me and Max outside of his room in Wilson showing off our matching guts. I think he got me by about two pounds.

Chapter 23

THIS MUST BE THE PART of the story where I tell you about the night not long ago when I was surfing the Internet, searching all the big-city newspaper archives and finding this obscure sports article, buried in the middle of the sports section. It was from the Baltimore, Maryland *Daily Herald*. The dateline was the first day of October in 1961:

Flame-Throwing Mystery Reliever
Slams Door on Birds

By A. J. Bentley
October 1, 1961
Baltimore, Maryland (UPI)

> *The Baltimore Orioles wrapped up the 1961 season yesterday, dropping a close one 4-3 to the visiting Chicago White Sox. Another third place finish for the O's again prompted fans to stay away in droves. Paid attendance for the last game of the season was 13,312 souls, an all-time low.*
>
> *Scoring all four of their runs in the top of the first off starter Milt Pappas, the White Sox capitalized on an error by the Orioles' rookie left fielder Boog Powell with two outs which extended the inning and led to Nellie Fox's three-run dinger, his 7th of the season. Chicago's next batter, light-hitting shortstop Luis Aparicio, hit a solo shot down the right field line that stayed fair long enough to clear the wall and the foul pole, giving the out-of-towners a 4-0 lead. After allowing a sharp*

single up the middle and then a walk, Pappas got White Sox pitcher Don Larsen to dribble a ground ball to first with two aboard to end the inning.

Neither team got a player past second base from the bottom of the first through the bottom of the ninth in this defensive gem of a ballgame. Both teams spread out four hits each during this stretch – all singles except for a double by Powell in the sixth. Pappas settled down after that shaky first inning and Larsen was sharp as ever on the mound for the White Sox. Had it not been for three miraculous plays turned in by the Orioles' third baseman Brooks Robinson, robbing three White Sox batters out of clean base hits, this one would have been akin to watching paint dry.

The game didn't get interesting again until the bottom of the ninth. Still down 4-0, Oriole leadoff batter Jim Gentile doubled off the wall in right center. Larsen, the Chicago starter, the guy who pitched a perfect game for the New York Yankees in the '56 World Series, looked as though his day was finished when he walked the next batter, on four straight pitches. After a brief visit to the mound from manager Al Lopez, Larsen was left in the game to pitch to the Orioles rightfielder, Whitey Herzog. Larsen owned Herzog, having struck him out in the first, fourth, and seventh.

But not this time. Herzog blasted Larsen's first pitch deep into the centerfield stands and brought the score to 4-3.

And this is where things took another interesting twist.

There were no stats – minor league or major league – or any other information available for the reliever Lopez brought in to pitch in this close, but otherwise meaningless ballgame at the end of a dismal season. Only his name was announced over the Memorial Stadium PA system. A search for information on this mystery pitcher after the game by this reporter proved futile.

This is all that is known for certain.

The reliever, identified as Max Mangum, took the ball from Lopez and threw ten warm-up pitches that resounded like gunshots in catcher Sherm Lollar's mitt. At this point in the game, most of the sparse crowd had already flooded to the exits and gone home, leaving fewer than three thousand fans in the seats. The very hard-throwing righty had everyone's attention though. On each of his warm-ups, it seemed that as soon as Mangum released the ball from his hand, dust immediately billowed from Lollar's mitt, followed immediately by the echoing gunshot sound.

There was a palpable buzz in the paltry crowd. As Lollar flexed and examined the fingers of his left hand, the talk in the stands was about the little white blur that was supposed to be a baseball. Larsen's fastball was estimated in the mid-ninety mile per hour range, but this Mangum character's heater was in a class all its own. It was not lost on this reporter that Lollar didn't move a muscle to catch Mangum's warm-ups.

With nobody out and the bases clean, Oriole left fielder Dick Williams stepped up to the plate. Mangum, who looked to be in his late twenties or early thirties, delivered three pitches, three blistering fastballs, in less than one minute and Williams slunk back to the dugout. His bat never left his shoulder. During his career, Dick Williams has been one of those hitters who follows the ball with his eyes and his head all the way to the mitt, even if the pitch is not a strike. It was clear that he was having trouble seeing and following the baseball. So was everyone else.

The big redheaded rookie power hitter, Boog Powell, batted next. Powell took his sweet time getting ready at the plate, trying to take Mangum out of his rhythm. It didn't work on the first pitch as Mangum's fastball streaked past the rookie and into the catcher's mitt for strike one. Powell stepped out of the box, scooped up some dirt, and looked down to his third base coach. At 249 pounds and slower than molasses on a mid-winter Minnesota morning, he wasn't likely to get the bunt sign. Powell must have figured the only chance he had at connecting with such a fastball was to start swinging as soon as Mangum released the ball. And on the second pitch, that's what he did. The problem was what he got was about a 50 mile per hour curve that Powell actually swung at twice! He missed both times.

Unprecedented in major league history, home plate umpire Del McNally called Powell out. His reasoning: three strikes. The game was delayed for several minutes while the Orioles' interim manager Lum Harris argued the call, but without much intensity. Powell's unorthodox strike out made it two down.

The Orioles' sensational young third baseman Brooks Robinson was up next, representing the last hope of a lost season. Robinson, batting .288 at the time, had an eleven-game hitting streak on the line. That's a long way from DiMaggio's 56-game record, but who knew? It's obvious this Robinson kid is destined for greatness for his glove play over on the hot corner at third. Maybe he had some magic in his bat as well.

White Sox catcher Lollar gave Mangum the sign and set up inside, holding the mitt at knee-high. Robinson, already notorious for crowding the plate, had a most severe look of determination on his face and actually dug in a little closer than usual.

Impossibly, Mangum reached back and got a little more on his already phenomenal fastball. The crowd was dead silent and the only evidence of a pitch was the quick, soft whistling 'sh' of the ball on its very brief trip to home plate and the sonic boom a split second later. Lollar didn't move his mitt to catch the strike that missed Robinson's left kneecap by less than an inch. Robinson flinched about two seconds too late. The pitch painted the inside corner and the paint was dry by the time Lollar returned the ball to Mangum.

The sparse crowd at Memorial Stadium was really into it now. They knew they were seeing something special, something that had never been seen before. Most baseball people know that Cleveland's Bob Feller was the hardest throwing pitcher ever to wear a major league uniform. With the help of the U.S. Army Corps of Engineers, it was determined that Feller's fastball hit a top speed of 103 miles per hour. This reporter has seen Feller pitch and knows what a 103 mph fastball looks like. And it didn't look anything like this. Mangum's heater is in a league of its very own, no doubt. This reporter is simply estimating, but Mangum's fastball was moving at least ten mph faster than Bob Feller's. A batter's reaction time to a 100 mph pitch is four-tenths of a second; not a lot of time to swing. At 110-plus? Virtually no time.

Robinson, down 0-1 in the count, must have figured he was going to see Mangum's little curve that had destroyed Powell just a few minutes earlier. He figured wrong. If Mangum's first pitch was 110, this one had to have been a little more. Lollar, who'd set up dead center of the plate and holding his mitt straight out in front of him, found himself lying in the arms of the umpire as both were blown back by the force and velocity of Mangum's fastball. Again, Robinson's flinch was a few seconds too late.

Lollar returned the ball to Mangum, who inexplicably walked around to the back of the mound and slammed his glove in the dirt. He stood there rubbing the baseball with his bare hands for a few minutes until the umpire, McNally, yelled at him to, "Play ball!"

Mangum picked up his glove and toed the pitching rubber. Robinson dug in for the 0-2 pitch. This reporter cannot be sure if this third pitch to Robinson was faster than the previous two, but he is certain that it wasn't any slower. A loud POP, a very late and very ugly swing, and nearly three thousand fans at home in Baltimore were cheering a Chicago White Sox pitcher for shutting down their team in the final inning.

Who is this Max Mangum character and where did he come from? This reporter was not successful in discovering a single piece of information on this 'phantom of the bullpen' from the White Sox players, coaches, or the manager. Each of those who were interviewed after the game replied, "No comment." Mangum could not be found. He had disappeared.

Folks, it doesn't get much more mysterious than that.

In a halfway more perfect world, this, or something similar to it, might have happened. But, as you surely must know by now from experience, if not by witness, this is not a perfect world. Not even halfway.

I sincerely apologize if this fictional account has upset the reader. I just wanted to see what this kind of situation would look like on paper and sound like in my ears when I read it out loud. For whatever reason, as I wrote it and read it aloud, I was hearing the voice of Mel Allen all the way through. And after rereading it many times, what I've always thought of as The Voice of Baseball is still there.

There's something to be said for nostalgia, even if it's conjured up nostalgia.

I guess I did this fictional part just to satisfy my selfishness, but I hope anyone who reads it, enjoys it in the manner in which it was offered. It's simply a gift for Max that he'll never receive.

I struggled with this fictional concept because I had worked so hard to keep every word of Phantom of the Bullpen true and tell the story as it happened. Again I succumbed to selfishness. I did some research on the Orioles and the White Sox from that year and the rest was easy.

Since it was a fictional account, I may have stretched a little too far with Boog Powell's 2-pitch, 3-swing strikeout. I have no idea how an umpire would handle such a situation. "Da rule book says dat ya gets three strikes, not three pitches, big fella. Yer outta there!"

I want to apologize once again for the fictional account and for not giving the reader some kind of heads-up to prepare for the letdown. I would like to attempt to make up for it with the next chapter. The next chapter includes an absolutely true newspaper account I stumbled across.

Within the scope of this story, it is truly epic.

The following chapter in no way validates the claims I've made throughout this story as to how phenomenal a pitcher Max Mangum could have been. It does, however, prove just what kind of man Max Mangum was. The next chapter gives us a glimpse of the internal drive of a man who. if given half a chance, could possibly have become a Hall of Fame pitcher, joining the ranks of Walter Johnson, Dizzy Dean, Cy Young and all the other greats.

But Max Mangum was never given a chance.

No chance at all.

Chapter 24

Back in the summer of 1976, Max was 46 years old, out of shape, living alone, and dealing with paranoid schizophrenia the same way the rest of us deal with breathing – every moment of every day. Sometime in the middle of June that year, Max discovered that there was going to be a major league tryout at Harding High School in Charlotte, North Carolina on Saturday morning, June 26.

Late Friday night on June 25, Max boarded a Trailways bus at the West Jones Street station in Raleigh. After a dozen or so little stops along the way, he rolled into Charlotte Saturday morning with his glove on his hand, his spikes hanging over his shoulder, and in his heart, a heaping helping of major league dreams. I have no doubt it was that way every time Max ventured to a pro tryout. He was always sitting on dead-ready to throw a baseball. That day, just like every other tryout day, Max was the first guy on the field.

On the next page are a couple of photos from an article that appeared in the Sunday edition of the Charlotte Observer on June 27, 1976. If the reader would like to view and read the original article, go to Newspapers.com and type in the name Gaius Max Mangum. You may have to pay a small fee, unless you're lucky like me.

An Ambition That Won't Go Away…

Gaius Max Mangum, 46, isn't so different from the other men with gloves, baseball shoes and hopeful expressions who show up at major league tryout camps like the one held in Charlotte Saturday. He's just a little older. Like the two dozen others who showed up at Harding High School, he didn't get a contract.

Gaius Max Mangum Fires His Best Pitch . . .

. . And Jumps For Line-Drive Result

Tryout Camp: 5 Minutes From A Dream's End

By BOB CLARY
Observer Sports Writer

"Lemme tell ya about this kid." Cigar smoke swirls from a confident puff. "This kid can do it all. He has talent. He has the power of Frank Howard, the fastball of Sandy Koufax, the speed of Maury Wills. Somebody oughta take a look at him."

Guys like Bill Jamieson, Jim Gruzdis, they've heard those lines more times than they can count. And, invariably, they do take a look. That's their job. They scout baseball talent as part of a central scouting agency for the major league teams.

Usually, a look is all they need. "I can tell in five minutes if you have what we're looking for" Jamieson told a group of two dozen hopefuls Saturday morning at Harding High School, site of one of the 19 tryout camps he will hold this summer.

For some, five minutes is more than enough. For others, more looks are needed. Such was the contrast offered by a couple of pitchers Saturday, by Gaius Max Mangum and Dean Reavis.

Gaius Max Mangum is 46 years old. He caught a bus from Raleigh, then took a cab to the field. He also had to take a bus ride home. Sure you have to get up early, he said, but shoot. "This'll get you so nervous you can't sleep the night before, anyway."

So there was Gaius Max Mangum out there with the kids. Of course, he was snickered at. "I was throwing pretty good yesterday," he said. "But I was wild down

See TRYOUT Page 4B, Col. 1

Seriously. I hope you're question right now is, "Allen, how did you get to this point?"

Good question.

John Lennon once said, "Life is what happens when you are busy making other plans." It's a simple, poignant concept, really. It just means that life goes on whether you're aware of what's going on or not.

Time truly waits for no one and it won't wait for me, you, or anyone else.

Again, I'll try to be brief.

I never saw Max again after visiting him at the Brian Center in 2008. Life got in the way. I was just too busy. In 2012, I got busy losing the house I'd bought at Lake Royale in 2004. I got busy in 2015 coaching both the men's and women's tennis teams at Bunn High School, and I got busy getting fed up enough with the direction education was going to retire from teaching in 2017.

And I thought I would teach forever.

I also thought I would have gotten this story published by then, but things don't always work out like a simple-minded fellow like me thinks they ought to.

I could never find a literary agent because my query letters sucked. I couldn't afford to self-publish because teachers in North Carolina didn't get a raise from 2007 to 2013 and, the real truth, I'm just not that good with managing money. Why do you think I married an accountant? Just kidding again. I manage to get the bills paid, but the rest I squander foolishly on fuel: food, gasoline, and cigarettes.

In February of 2021, I was totally fed up with all the Covid bullshit, so I decided to try yet again to find a literary agent and get Phantom of the Bullpen published. It's a great story! Not because I wrote it, but because it's a great story! I know that every baseball fan who reads it is going to enjoy it. It's a slam dunk, or maybe a grand slam would be more appropriate but Max is a pitcher and 'strike out' doesn't fit, and neither does 'homerun' so it's a slam dunk!

I also got to work writing a good, full revision of the story, adding some cool things I'd remembered, and coloring some things that needed more detail. At the same time I was emailing better-crafted query letters to about 30 agents scattered about the country. Eventually, I received standard rejection letters from most of the agents. But three or four sent personalized messages saying 'great idea for a story' and 'good luck' and 'like your writing style' and my parting response before deleting them was always just the standard one word: Shit.

Chris Lewis, a former colleague and now the Athletic Director at Bunn High School, hooked me up with someone his sister knew in Durham who worked with Baseball America and somehow that led me to August Publications, but, in the end, that didn't work out either. Close, but no hot dog. I thought I had a very good chance with them, but it just didn't happen.

Sometime in March of 2021 while working on my revision, I decided to take a break and find out how Max was doing. The number I had for Suzanne Landis was no longer any good, so I just did another Google search using Max's name. I was hoping I'd get a chance to go see him again and I'd go by myself this time if I had to. I was all grown up now at almost 66 years old. And Max, he had to be pushing 90. We had a lot of catching up to do.

And then you get shot right out of the saddle.

Max Mangum died at the Brian Center in Wilson, North Carolina at the age of 87 on Friday, June 9, 2017. I read the obituary two or three times but the sad news stayed the same. For a moment or two, I felt very alone in the world. I was hurt beyond measure, but then I realized that Max wasn't lying in hospital bed any longer and he no longer had to deal with paranoid schizophrenia. I can't say that I was happy, but I did feel an overwhelming sense of relief for him. He was now able to stand on equal footing with the likes of Babe Ruth, Joe DiMaggio, and Ted Williams. Max is finally getting his chance.

But Max was gone and I was left holding his story. I can't hold it for much longer.

Something has to give.

Instead of making up another newspaper article, I thought I'd see if I could find a real one. Just a little something to balance out the fictitious account I wrote earlier. I logged into Newspapers.com and gave it a shot. Unfortunately, they wanted money to let me in and I didn't have any of that.

I had a thousand used tennis balls, but I also had a feeling they wouldn't be interested in a trade.

I said to myself, *F-'em,* or something similar to that. I may have even said it out loud. I'm a bad boy sometimes.

I went through the motions anyway, just to see how much it would cost. I plugged in my information: name, address, email, phone number, etc. and then politely backed out (hit the X) when I saw how much it would cost. Yes, I said it again. This time very loudly. I don't remember what day of the week it was when I tried Newspapers.com, but I got an email from them on Friday informing me of their promotional Free Weekend starting that day! I don't think you can un-f somebody, but I did kind of apologized to them in my mind.

I typed in Max's name and struck pure gold.

And that's how I got to this point.

While reading the article, I came across another reason why Max believed that I was a scout for the Pittsburgh Pirates. Yes, we named our Men's Senior Baseball League team the Zebulon Pirates because of the new stadium and the minor league team coming to town was a farm team of the big league Pirates. But I think one of the scouts there that day in 1976 may have had a subconscious impact on Max of which he was not aware.

Besides Bill Jamieson and Jim Gruzdis, there was another scout on the scene searching for some major league talent. You may or may not have ever heard of him, but if you're a baseball fan, I'm sure you've heard of his grand-father: Branch Rickey. Mr. Rickey is best known for being the man who signed Jackie Robinson to a big league contract with the Brooklyn Dodgers in 1947, and thus breaking the color barrier in Major League Baseball. There were other folks involved in making that piece of MLB history happen, but Branch Rickey is the man most readily identified as the driving force.

Branch Rickey III, his grandson, was a hard-working big league scout during the 70s and 80s, traveling the United States from city to city, town to town, crossroad to crossroad, looking under every rock, going deep into coal mines, scouring the edges of tobacco fields, and checking out every rumor about some exceptional baseball player. When he wasn't doing that, he was participating in various publicized major league tryouts all over the country, hoping to find the next Bob Gibson, Mickey Mantle, or uh, Cliff Johnson.

Mr. Rickey III was a very busy man during this time, and like the article says, the good scouts can spot a kid in about five minutes who has the right stuff to at least have a chance to play professional baseball.

Key word: kid.

It appears from the comments in the article that Jamieson and Gruzdis appreciated the novelty of a 46-year old man trying to break into 'The Show' but even one with a serious heater isn't going to get any consideration. Especially if he's carrying around a bushel basket overflowing with weird quirks. Max never really had much of a chance to get into the big leagues after his mid-20's, but it would have been a major league waste of breath trying to tell *him* that.

The article goes on to mention that after the tryout had ended and no contracts were offered, Branch Rickey III had given Max a ride from Harding High School to the bus station in Charlotte so he could return home.

Bingo!

I thought this was the break I was looking for to get a little more insight into Max during this time of his life. With nothing to lose except time, I put Branch Rickey III's name in my computer and Googled him every which way but loose. And then, as always, I leaped before I looked closely.

The most recent information I could find on BRIII told me that he was the president of the Pacific Coast League. I had a good feeling that a fellow like me may just be able to find a fellow with a high profile job like that.

I Googled the Pacific Coast League, not bothering to notice any dates. Spotting Mr. Rickey's email address, I composed a nice little letter and sent it along its merry way, absolutely sure that I'd hear back from the excited executive within an hour, just dying to tell me all about his morning with Max forty-five years ago.

Okay, maybe tomorrow.

Sometime this week?

Where did I go wrong? I mean, other than getting up this morning.

At this exact time, I was also in contact with Kevin Reichard at August Publications about getting Phantom of the Bullpen published. AP publishes *Ballpark Digest* and *Spring Training Online*. They have also published some great sports books as well. Most notably, and the latest, is Andy Strasberg's *My 1961*, which chronicles Strasberg's life in and around New York City, but mainly his 13th year, which was the year Roger Maris broke Babe Ruth's homerun record – 1961. Although I was only six in 1961, Strasberg's story was an emotional rollercoaster ride for me and I highly recommend 'My 1961' to all baseball fans.

Believe it or not, Mr. Reichard and I connected on Facebook! No shit! I sent a private message and he responded. I should take a screenshot and stick it in here somewhere. Na. No need to glorify a lost cause.

He requested and I sent him the first eight chapters of the story, he read it, and then he emailed me back. He told me he liked my writing style and then said, "But I gotta ask: how are you going to prove this guy threw in the 90s in his 60s?"

What? You don't believe me?

Mr. Reichard then wrote that, "At first read, this is a Sidd Fitch kinda tale…" I had no idea who Sidd Fitch was so I did a little research on this Sidd kid.

Sidd Fitch was a fictional character developed for Sports Illustrated by George Plimpton for a timely April Fools Day edition of SI in 1985. (I've seen 'Fools' written with and apostrophe after the s, between the l and the s, and without an apostrophe. I prefer without simply because it saves just this much ink – ' – if you don't use it. Thank me later for this economical tip; I'm kind of busy right now.

Sorry. I am so easily distracted.

I guess I can see Mr. Reichard making the connection to the Sidd Fitch hoax because of the April 1st similarity in the two stories, but a claim of someone throwing a baseball 168 miles per hour is obviously absurd. It's simply not humanly possible. Yet. At one time, running the 100m dash in less than 10 seconds wasn't possible until Usain Bolt did it.

Never say never and all that jazz fusion.

Mr. Reichard may know a lot about baseball, but Phantom of the Bullpen is NOTHING like the Sidd Fitch bullshit. Nor is it a tale.

I emailed him back, but I didn't say what was going through my mind at the time. I couldn't say that I just wasn't equipped to video my random encounter with the stranger because it was, uh, so random and, on top of that, I had no idea what kinda shit was about to go down. I also didn't need to mention the fact that phones with cameras were not in the public domain in 1991. Mr. Reichard knew that as well as I did.

My ace in the hole was and is the video I have of Max throwing to me at his Shade Stadium, but it was taken a few years after our initial meeting in October of 1991. Max's velocity had fallen off a little bit, but he was still throwing the ball, then at the age of sixty-four, somewhere between 83-87mph. I was sure that I'd mentioned this video to Mr. Reichard in my reply, but in late August as I reread our correspondence hoping to get August Publications to give Phantom of the Bullpen another look, I discovered that I did not.

The man asked me one important question and I flat out failed to answer it.

I can hear Stacy Overman now, *"Shoot yourself in the foot much, White?"*

I did, however, throw in my wild card and informed Mr. Reichard about finding the article from the Charlotte Observer that featured Max in the Newpaper.com archives. Being rather proud of locating Mr. Rickey via the Internet, I also mentioned to him in the email that Branch Rickey III, who was a scout for the Pittsburgh Pirates, was one of the three men conducting the tryout that day in 1976. I let him know that Mr. Rickey III was the was the president of the Pacific Coast League and that I'd just sent *him* an email asking if he remembered anything about Max's performance that day in 1976, and that 'I should be hearing from him anytime now.'

Mr. Reichard of August Publications emailed back me a little later that same day. He told me that there was no longer a Pacific Coast League and that it had been bought out by Major League Baseball. *Well, excuuuuse me,* I thought. *I didn't get the memo.* At the time, I didn't know just how firmly Mr. Reichard had his thumb on the pulse of major and minor league baseball.

He then wrote that he would ask 'Branch' about Max when he saw him. *Well, excuuuuse me again! We should all be so darn connected.* Just kidding.

I wasn't really upset at Mr. Reichard or anyone else. I was just disappointed at yet another strikeout. That was the last I heard from Mr. Reichard and this was just another sad little saga that I was going to have to put behind me.

A week or two later, guess who received an email from Mr. Branch Rickey III? This guy! That's who!

Call me anal retentive, but I keep that sucker alive as 'new' mail on my computer. (I just checked; it's still there.)

Mr. Rickey apologized (to me!) for taking so long to respond and gave me a few reasons for doing so that were perfectly legit. He then apologized for not remembering a single thing about Max or anyone else that day in Charlotte. As I continued to read the email, I discreetly placed another hunk of major disappointment into my far-too-handy 'Just My Luck' file.

Some things never change.

Mr. Rickey said that he was a very busy man during that time, which I already knew, and there were a lot of people and places that he just couldn't remember. He didn't even remember giving Max a ride from Harding High School to the bus station when the tryout ended.

But he was kind enough to respond to my mother-of-all Hail Mary attempts to find out some solid intel on my Phantom of the Bullpen. I was hoping with every atom of my being that he was going to remember Max and give me a boatload of great quotes to put right here, but as you can see, the rest of this page is blank.

Chapter 25

THIS IS NOT QUITE THE ENDING I wanted for this story, but like the Rolling Stones song says, You Can't Always Get What You Want. I wanted to include interviews from a few of Max's Wake Forest Hight School contemporaries to spice up a chapter or two and I tried hard to find them, believe me, I tried.

A word or two from a couple of his high school teammates would have surely kicked the story up a notch or two, also. And I just knew that the pleasant, smiling kid with the wavy hair and the flaming-hot fastball was bound to have a gal or three interested in him. Maybe I'd get a steamy quote from one of Max's old girlfriends to add a little romance to the story.

Hey. Ya never know.

I visited the librarian at Wake Forest High School during the middle of the COVID-19 pandemic with hopes of getting a look at the yearbooks from Max's high school days. My intent was to visit the library itself, but they wouldn't let me in the school. Oh, I could have gotten in if I'd wanted to, but I have no desire to be a headline in the news at 4 or a footer running across the bottom of the screen on CNN.

The librarian met me outside and told me they had yearbooks on the shelf from the 30's on through last year, but there was a gap in the coverage and that gap included the four years that Max would have passed through there. Yeah. I know. Just my luck.

Then I remembered that a former colleague from Bunn Middle School, Corey Hutcherson, had left the teaching profession about ten years ago to work with the town of Wake Forest and I contacted him for some help. After explaining the situation to him, he said, "So, you want me to find some elderly people around here who may have been in high school with this guy from

1945 through 1948?" When he put it that way, I could see just how thin my hopes were.

I thought about it for a second and said, "Yes, that's about the size of it, Corey. Can you help me out?"

"You know it's 2021, right?"

I mocked a surprise look, but he wasn't fooled. He knew me too well.

Corey said, "Sure. No problem. I'll get back with you as soon as I find a candidate."

It's been six months now, and I still haven't heard back from my friend. I tried a few other avenues as well, but those roads were also closed.

Yeah. I know. Just my luck. Hey, I'm just as tired of saying it as you are reading it.

I don't like it, but I have finally come to grips with the fact that I can't always get what I want. No amount of whining and crying or wishing and trying is going to change that. I do believe, though, even with the subpar, shoddy, and unprofessional research that I was able to accomplish, I did, in fact, get enough to tell Max's story.

It will be left up to the reader to determine if I am correct.

My one and only hope and desire is that I've gotten across the point of this story. Mr. Gaius "Max" Mangum was a truly unique individual who had so much to offer the world, but paranoid schizophrenia neutralized that gift, rendering it impossible to share. To stare frustration dead in the eye every day the way Max did, and still push on toward his desired goal against a host of invisible and insurmountable odds is simply incredible and almost unbelievable. I probably wouldn't have believed it if I hadn't witnessed it myself.

I think that it has somehow been left up to me to help him share his inspiring story with others, and I am humbled and honored to be that bridge. I'm still trying. Often I think of the influence Max had on me and my life. Where would I be now if I hadn't met him that day back in October of 1991?

Damn good question.

I shudder to think.

Whether I taught language arts or social studies, I always managed to work Max and an appropriate version or excerpt of this story into our course of study. I told my students that if it had not been for my chance meeting of this man, I wouldn't be standing there talking to them. All good learning does not come from the curriculum.

I hate to be so cliché, but everything happens for a reason. And honestly, I don't know where I would have ended up, or what I would have done, if I hadn't crossed paths with Max Mangum.

Because of my relationship with Max, I was able to have positive and meaningful relationships with many hundreds, perhaps thousands, of students, athletes, and their parents during my twenty-five years in education. Many of them still ask about Max and they also ask if I've gotten the story published yet. "No, not yet," I say. "Maybe someday."

Someday. I guess this is where we hear John Fogerty and Creedence Clearwater Revival singing again. This time they're singing the saddest song ever.

Someday Never Comes.

For various and sundry reasons, I've been sitting on this story for a long, long time. It's still not completely finished, but this is the best I could do with a 30-year deadline hanging over my head. Just kidding, still. I don't think it will ever be complete.

As I said, Max Mangum died in the hospital in Wilson on June 9th, 2017. I truly regret that I did not get to visit him during his final few years. I regret even more that I didn't learn of his death until four years after the fact. That same hectic, random, and spontaneous life that brings us together sometimes keeps us apart as well.

Max's ability to pitch a baseball with such velocity and accuracy well into his sixth decade was nothing short of phenomenal. The crux of this story, though, is about me trying to find out just how hard he was throwing that thing when he was fifty-three. What about forty-three? Or thirty-three? How about twenty-three?

That's the one thing I could never determine for sure, so it all comes down to conjecture and speculation. I can get close, based on the facts as I know them, but anyone else's theory would probably be just as good as mine. Everybody is an expert on everything these days, or haven't you noticed?

One truth I discovered on this odyssey is that there never seems to be a JUGS gun around when you need one.

I have to do some back-projecting, but I figure if Max could throw the ball 85-90 miles per hour in his mid-sixties (and he could and I have it on film), it only stands to reason that he was throwing much harder when he was younger. I mean, he destroyed wooden sheds on his farm with his fastball! Accepting that fact, then 100 miles per hour at age thirty-three would be on the low end of the guess spectrum.

Think about that for a minute.

Seriously. Think about it.

I hate to admit this, but there were a few times that I got to wondering if it was actually *me* who was the Phantom of the Bullpen. From how deep out in left field did an off-the-wall thought like that have to come? There's no telling, but the thought was there. I figure I could have played major league baseball had it not been for a thousand little 'ifs' scattered about in my overall equation. There was only one 'if' in Max Mangum's equation, but it was the biggest 'if' ever. *If* he hadn't had paranoid schizophrenia, where would his strong right arm and his precision pitching ability have taken him?

I honestly believe that if he hadn't been a paranoid schizophrenic, the name Max Mangum would have become a household name as early as the 1950's and would still be one to this day.

Also, I honestly wish I could have seen Max pitch in his prime, from the stands, that is, or from my position in leftfield or first base. Would fielders have even be necessary with Max on the mound in his prime? Probably not.

Move over Satchel Paige.

I've always loved hitting the baseball, but even if I knew ahead of time about his unfathomable control, I still would *not* want to be anywhere near the batter's box with Gaius Max Mangum standing on the mound.

You can't hit what you can't see.

One more thing. No, two. If there IS a rock and roll Heaven, well, I'm certain they have a hell of a band. And if they play baseball in Heaven, I know who's starting on the mound tonight for the good guys.

Max Mangum.

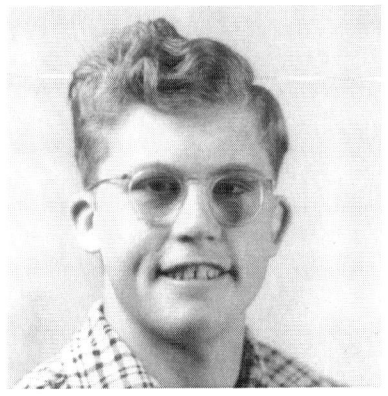

The Phantom Chapters

I FEEL THE NEED TO CLARIFY some things here about myself and share some of the highlights and lowlights of my early life. It's ok, though. There is no charge or any hidden fees. The official story is over. You can stop now if you wish, but I hope you will continue to read until the end. It would be a stretch, but you could call it free baseball, like when a game goes into extra innings.

Originally, these following three chapters were in the middle of *Phantom of the Bullpen* as Chapters 13, 14, and 15. They kind of fit there, but their length created a lull in the flow of the story and didn't really do much to move the story forward. Max didn't exist to me during the timeframe of these three chapters and that caused a major speedbump that shouldn't have been there.

So I took them out.

My goal was to make the story flow more smoothly for the reader. Max is still the main character in this part of the story, too, but there is nothing about him in these three chapters. The very thin link or connection between Max and me during this time would be the silent frustration that we both were suffering, but my pain wasn't even in the same ballpark as his.

Neither of us was capable of changing our circumstances. Sometimes, there is simply nothing you can do to alter your environment except hang on, keep the faith, and believe that one day everything will work out for the best. There is a big difference between giving up and giving a bad situation a chance to work itself out.

Although it was difficult to put some of these truths about me out there, overall this was a largely cathartic experience.

There may be a passage or two of social commentary contained within the following three chapters as well. Drugs and alcohol are mentioned also, but in no way, shape, or form am I glorifying the use, abuse, or misuse of them. I'm just telling things like they were.

Also included here are some of the more bizarre happenings on the baseball field during my high school days. I played well most of the time and enjoyed some personal success and accolades, but our team didn't win many baseball games. Last time I looked, baseball was still a team sport.

It's a good feeling to strike out 15 guys from the other team.

It's a good feeling to give up only 3 or 4 legitimate hits against a strong lineup.

It's a good feeling to rip a bases loaded triple and get three ribbies.

All those things would give any baseball player a good feeling, but when you lose that same game on runs scored by guys who shouldn't have even been on base, it creates a hollow good feeling. Very hollow. It has no substance to it. There is something missing.

The win.

The good and bad thing about memories is that they don't care if you win or lose.

Memories are forever.

I would much rather have given a more extensive accounting of Max's early life in the middle of this story, but I didn't have it. Other than some great recollections from Max's sister, two of his cousins, and Phil Johnson of Johnson-Lambe Sporting Goods, I found virtually no one else who could offer any information about his youth.

Sadly, that bus left the station a long time ago.

Oh, I love writing fiction and could have made up an incredibly convincing load of bullshit involving Max, his early days, and his infinite love and mastery of pitching, but I wanted to keep this story 100% true. I also believe that the reader prefers the truth as opposed to something fabricated to fill space. I could be wrong and that would be familiar territory for me, but I decided to stick with truth, the whole truth, and nothing but the truth, so help me God.

So, help me, God!

deleted Chapter 13

MY GRANDFATHER, JESSE WHITE, suffered a fatal heart attack one morning while shoveling snow from our walkway in January of 1964. I was in my third grade classroom that morning when the principal of Van Grade School, Willard Peele, came into the room. He came in every morning to collect lunch money and other funds (the original thug, he was) so I hardly noticed him. At the moment, I was in my seat and not bothering anyone, which was rare, so I continued to pay him no mind. I think I was looking at a Highlights book or something akin to it.

On this particular morning, after fleecing me and my classmates, Mr. Peele announced to the class, "I will be collecting flower money tomorrow for Jesse White who passed away earlier this morning."

That got my undivided attention in a hurry. I realized, even at that age, that I was being raised by my grandparents, but to me, they were Mommy and Daddy. My teacher, Mrs. Barker, seemed more shocked by this news than I was. Her mouth fell open and her clinched right fist covered it up immediately. Whatever she was going to say never made it past her hand. Mr. Peele paused halfway to the door and said, "Oh, I think his grandson is in this class. Allen?"

Even though it was January in West Virginia with a fresh, eight-inch snowfall on the ground and the red mercury in the classroom thermometer just outside the window leveled off at just below the 30 mark, I'd have to say *that* move was still pretty damned cold. I put my head down on my desk and cried, waiting for someone to come get me.

The next three years were kind of tough. It seems there was big hole in the Social Security net, but I was too young to understand the problem. My grandfather was only 57 when he died, perhaps that was the hang-up. I just don't know. He also had emphysema and black lung. Working in a coal mine from age 14 will do that to you.

Rex had to give up his scholarship at New Mexico Highlands to come home and help Mike support me and my grandmother. Things got better and we were going along ok, but in 1966, Rex was drafted into the Army. Bill had served in the Army and Clifford had served in the Navy, so Rex followed in the footsteps of his older brothers to serve his country.

In 1967, while stationed in France during the Vietnam conflict, Rex met a girl from North Carolina. Anne Creech was a lovely Southern Belle and after a year-long courtship, they fell in love and were married in her hometown of Zebulon. My grandmother, Marie, traveled south to attend the wedding and must have liked the area well enough to move us there a year later.

It was just the two of us by that time. Mike had already moved to North Carolina and had a job working as a knitting machine mechanic in the textile factory where Rex was the quality control manager. I later found out that my grandmother moved us to Zebulon from her home of sixty-some years just to get me out of Van, West Virginia, where she thought the possibilities of any kind of future for me were virtually nonexistent. She did not want me to be a coal miner.

We moved to the great state of North Carolina in April of 1969. I was in the eighth grade and had just turned fourteen in March. That summer, I played Pony League baseball and did very well, thanks to Mike showing me yet a better way of gripping my curveball. I already had a good curve and a good 'drop' ball, but when Mike showed me how to cock my forefinger back and snuggle that last joint tight to the threads on the ball, it added a much sharper break to both pitches. I was recognized as Player-of-the-Week twice that summer and got my first taste of publicity and a big picture of myself on the sports page of the Zebulon Record, the town's weekly newspaper, looking about as goofy as a kid could look. Why do you think I made the picture so small?

Little League Baseball Player Of The Week

Allen White has the distinction of being the only Little League player to be chosen twice for Player of the Week. Allen has good pitching ability and really puts himself into each pitch. As a side-line, gets up two hits, and struck out two against Point in the final game of the season.

TEAM MANAGERS

PETE BRYANT
LAWRENCE LILES
MARK WILSON
W. G. GRISWOLD

MORGAN DRUG

Four months after that picture was taken, that goofy looking 14-year old kid with the big duck feet found himself starting at quarterback for the Wakelon High School Bulldogs a game or two near the end of the season. Our JV team played a 7-game schedule that fall and when our season was over, we joined up with the varsity team. If only I'd known what I was doing. I think I was the originator of and poster boy for the word *clueless.*

I didn't like playing football all that much, but I loved to throw the thing and I could remember the plays, so the position was mine. I was scared shitless most of the time and had no idea about the 'big picture' the quarterback is supposed to see. Bart Starr and Joe Namath made it look so easy and glamorous on television! All I could see was that the chicks really dug guys who were on the football team and that was motivation enough for me. How the hell I made all-conference my junior year, I'll never know.

In that 1969-70 school year, my freshman year, I came in with all of three games of junior high football under my belt from the fall before we moved. I had played a lot of football with my friends in the alley growing up in Y&O Coal Camp, but two-hand touch, as rough as we were sometimes, is one hell of a quantum leap to smashmouth tackle football.

I didn't know how to hit nor how to get hit, and there is a ton of hitting in football. My coaches were always protecting me at practice because I was a quarterback, and believe me, I was thankful for the don't-hit-the-QB status. On the other hand though, that false sense of security didn't do me a whole lot of good when we squared off against other schools. They had no such restrictions and I think KILL THE QUARTERBACK was their go-to slogan.

At the end of my sophomore year, during the final week of practice for the last game of the season, I finally figured it out. I learned how to hit and more importantly, I learned how to take a hit. In order to do it right, you have to be super aggressive and be the one who initiates contact. You have to be the one delivering the blows.

A perfect example would be Walter Payton. When Walter had done all he could do and gained as many yards as possible on the carry, and he knew he was going down, he was able to reach back and get a little something extra out of himself and literally punish his tackler for being there. And to toss a little salt onto the wounds he no doubt opened up, Walter Payton would jump up, seemingly as the whistle was still blowing, and be in the offensive huddle before his targets could scape themselves up off the field.

Take that, you dirty rat.

I could write a book about how wrong football is for allowing all the glory to go to the wrong guys. The guys who deserve to have their names and photos in the newspapers and magazines are the guys in the trench, in the box, in the perpetual hell known as the line of scrimmage. I'm talking about the center, the two guards, and the two tackles on offense. Those guys hit and get hit on every single play. I always felt guilty about getting the undeserved attention while my linemen, bloodied and bruised from head to toe, stood just outside the limelight.

Some things in life just aren't fair.

The 'tough guy' persona that went along with being a football player was a nice touch, but the 'dumb jock' stigma kind of pissed me off. One shouldn't simply assume that one is stupid because one plays football. That is blatant stereotyping and totally unacceptable.

Give me half a minute and I'll prove my stupidity all on my own merit.

I played football through my junior year, but my senior year on the gridiron was not to be. Taking advantage of a connection with my classmate, football teammate, and good friend John Zebulon Davis, I was able to get a few pointers from former UNC quarterback Paul Miller (a relative of JZD) during the summer of 1972. John and I also used our yearbook to recruit guys for the team because our roster was down to about 12 players at the end of our junior season. Things were really looking up for our senior season.

It was all for naught, though. We were expecting thirty or more guys, but only about eight came out for the first day of practice. Two of the eight were John and me. That was ok, though. Extra-curricular activities began taking up way too much of my time and none of them were even remotely related to school. There were too many things not jiving right on the football scene, so I didn't go back after that first practice.

I'm sorry. That's a lie. I did go back, but it's just difficult to talk about. I'll be as brief as possible.

For some reason, head football coach Mel Braswell did not return for his second year at the helm. There were rumors as to why, but they mattered little. We didn't have a coach the first day of practice! A week or so later, Leary Davis, John's older brother and local attorney, offered to coach the team, and suddenly, the team had a leader.

I still didn't care that much for the game of football, but I wasn't going to leave my teammates hanging. I showed up for the Tuesday practice of the third week of the season and was ready to rock and roll. I saw Lear– Coach Davis walking toward me and I figured he was coming to welcome me back to the team.

Not so fast, there, Quick Draw McGraw.

Coach Davis got between me and the guys I was talking to and looked me dead in the eye. He said, "You need to get a haircut if you want to play football." And with that, he turned and walked away.

Good thing I was wearing a chinstrap or my jaw would have fallen off my face. John's hair was longer than mine! Two or three other guys on the team had hair longer than mine. Many years later, John told me that Leary was just testing me to see if I was committed to the team. Well, I probably would have done anything Coach Davis said, *except* get a haircut. Hair doesn't have a thing to do with playing football or any other sport as long as it's not a factor in your performance. Look at some of the professional athletes on the fields and courts these days. How do you think dreads would have gone over in 1972?

The truth is that I was caught between being a half-assed hippie and a half-assed jock. Nobody likes a half-ass anything, so I chose. And chose wrong. I left practice a minute later and I did NOT go back again. That was a decision I've regretted every day for fifty years.

Why couldn't football be simple?

Like baseball!

One of the best things about playing baseball was that I didn't have to wear twenty pounds of hard plastic and foam padding. Baseball's a more natural game. My freshman year, I made the varsity baseball team. This was the final year for Wakelon High School because the following year, Wakelon would merge with the black high school in town, Shepard, to become Zebulon High School.

I think the state was a little behind on the desegregation plan, but I didn't really know a lot about the South and the southern brand of racism back then because I had just moved here. I was certainly no stranger to the ugliness of being racist and all I can say on my behalf is that I just didn't know any better at the time. With the help of God, I corrected that character flaw and became a better human being for it. I still have to remind myself of the basic principles of life occasionally, though. Nobody, and I mean nobody, is perfect.

I think we all know that.

The assassination of Dr. Martin Luther King, Jr., the riots in the big cities, and turning the fire hoses and German shepherds loose on black folks in the Deep South were things I'd seen on television, and I was appalled to say the least. But at the age of thirteen or fourteen, the only things real in life are the things you can touch and see. I hated to see people treated that way, but there was nothing I could do about it. I also hated that I was poor, had crooked teeth, and no daddy, but I couldn't do anything about that shit either.

I saw, heard, and witnessed petty racism during my first years in North Carolina and although I didn't agree with it and made covert attempts not to participate in it, I did nothing to stop it or slow it down either. Every single time it happened there was an opportunity for me to stand up against it and do the right thing, but I was always outnumbered, and being the new kid in town, I was still trying to fit in. The only place I wanted to be noticed was on the baseball field.

I say I was on the varsity baseball team, and I was, but I didn't get to play all that much. In reality, I don't have any recollection of playing in any game my freshman year.

Young Stars With Bat

Webb Overpowers Wakelon By 15-1

As luck and fate would have it, many years later, my dentist and very good friend, Merlin Young, remembered that his high school, Oxford Webb, played us during his senior year. He dug up a newspaper clipping from the game and pinned it prominently on the bulletin board in his waiting room. His name is mentioned in the headline and the story is mostly about him. My name is right there in the box score, though, highlighted in bright neon yellow, as having pitched an inning and serving up about 6 hits, two of which Merlin swears were his. They must have batted around on me if I gave up six hits and walked three, but my subconscious just won't let me go there. You can zoom in if you want to see the bloody results in black and white. Please don't.

At least I was throwing strikes.

I remain a bit miffed (not really) about Dr. Young's little shrine at my expense, but I'm sure as hell not going to say anything confrontational to a man who works with both of his hands inside my mouth while bracing both of his knees on my forehead. The fact that I was barely fifteen and he was at least seventeen or eighteen takes some of the sting from it. But not much.

Except for fellow freshmen Mark Chamblee, Jeff Price, and me, the rest of the guys on that team were all upperclassmen and pretty well entrenched in their positions. First baseman Jamie Pearce pitched one game during that season, but Earl Bunn was the team's main pitcher, and for good reason. He had a hard, nasty curveball and a sizzling fastball. Earl was basically unhittable and pitched twelve or thirteen of our games that year, except the few innings I threw in relief in the Oxford game, and possibly that one other game.

I, on the other hand, was very hittable at the time and our coach, Jimmy Harris proved it by letting me pitch batting practice every day. Perhaps that's what I thought I was doing when we played Oxford Webb. *Stupid freshman!* I recall several times Coach Harris hooking his arm around my neck and saying, "You're gonna be my ace next year, Allen."

Wow. I couldn't wait! I was going to be the ace of the pitching staff!

I was the ace all right. I was also the staff. I pitched every inning of every game for Zebulon High School in its first three years of existence. No, wait. That's not really true, either. In the middle of my junior season, a very good athlete named Terry Brayboy moved to Zebulon and he pitched two-thirds of the first inning in a home game against Clayton High School.

My arm was hurting from pitching back-to-back games on consecutive days and I told Coach Larry Matthews that I just couldn't go that day. Terry gave up nine painful runs due to walks, and with two outs in the top of the first, he had walked the bases full again. He was a damn good baseball player and faster than greased lightning in the field and on the bases, but he just couldn't find the plate. The fact that he tried told me a lot about his character.

Just our luck, he opted to go to Vaden Whitley High School a few miles away the following year. At this or any other time, I'll make no comment about Terry abandoning us for a 'better' school.

Traitor! *Oops. Did I say that out loud?*

So with two gone in the first, I called time-out and told Coach Matthews I would pitch the rest of the game. I remember nothing else about what happened during the game, but I do remember that we lost 9-2.

My sophomore pitching record was the same as the team's record: 2-12. For my junior year, my record was 1-12; the team was 1-13, the other loss going to Terry. My record and the team's record for my senior year was 0-14. Nothing like an Oh-fer to cap off your high school career. As I mentioned before, I averaged slightly more than ten strikeouts per game, but I don't think I pitched all those games because I was necessarily all that good. The real reason was because we had absolutely no one else who could throw strikes. I really didn't mind at all, though. I loved baseball and I loved being where the action is, and in baseball, if you're not at the plate with your big whoopin' stick, the mound is the place to be.

I made the all-conference team three years in a row and was voted Most Valuable Player by my teammates for those three years. I led the conference in hitting my sophomore year with a .461 batting average. Although I pitched well all three years, my hitting took a nosedive in the eleventh grade after some of my friends and I discovered Mary Jane and all her evil sisters, cousins, and assorted mutations. I think I may have hit close to .400 my junior year and I went 3 for 3 at the plate in the final game of my senior year to bring my batting average *up* to a mere .300. That's pitiful for high school baseball.

My best friend and third baseman on the team, Carey Strickland, could talk me into doing anything. Not '*just about anything*' but *absolutely* anything. And vice versa. From the day we met in study hall in September of our freshman year, it was Katie-bar-the-doors. Our relationship started out innocently enough, hinging on our mutual interests in sports, girls, and the taboo ideas about getting high.

Looking back now, I can clearly see that this was the beginning of the end of the innocence for me.

Funny thing, though, before we ever got high the first time, we were always laughing at someone or something. Usually we laughed at each other. I think we had a secret, unspoken contest going to see who could do the stupidest shit trying to make the other one laugh. The coup de grace was getting the other to spew food or drink, with extra points if it came out through the nose.

In class, Carey would roll up notebook paper and stick it in his ears and up his nose just to make me laugh. On at least three occasions that I know about, he took an M-80 and pushed the fuse through a burning cigarette down near the filter so it would go off inside the trashcan in the smoking area a few minutes later when we were safely back in class. Instead of taking notes in class, I would draw extremely anatomically incorrect naked mutants and leave them on somebody else's desk or put a handful of thumb tacks in some girl's chair.

Those are just a few of the things I feel comfortable sharing. Sorry, ladies. It was me.

The bottom line is that our relationship was always about laughing. If we could have realized right then and there, that, even with the aid of drugs and alcohol, nothing was going to get any funnier than it already was, or make us laugh any harder, perhaps we'd both have turned out differently. Hey, you can laugh only so hard. Getting a cramp in your diaphragm is probably the best you can hope to achieve.

Obviously, I did some things during my younger days that I shouldn't have. Who hasn't? First and foremost, I admit that I used and abused drugs and alcohol for more than ten years (1971-1982). News flash: I wasn't the first and I won't be the last.

An infinite number of studies have revealed myriad reasons why some people do this and others do not. Is it genetic or is it environmental or is it a combination of the two? Does it matter? No. The answers seem to get too ethical, technical, and complicated from this point on in all these studies and although much has changed over the years, one huge constant remains: people still use and abuse drugs and alcohol.

In my little mind, and that's all I have as a resource, it all comes down to one thing: making good decisions. I did not make good decisions. I questioned myself the first few times I was faced with what I knew were going to be life-changing choices, but apparently the interrogation was neither thorough enough nor sufficient enough to have much of an effect. After a while, the decision to do the wrong thing again and again was not much of a decision at all. Ernie Endorphin and Donnie Dopamine cleverly clouded and confused the decision-making process as the hook set deeper and deeper to where getting high became the automatic/default choice.

Samuel Johnson said, "The chains of habit are too weak to be felt until they are too strong to be broken." I guess that's why his Wikipedia page is two yards long. The man knew what he was talking about.

Mathematical ignoramus that I am, I came up with an equation that defines the illegal drug problem in its purest form:

$$Mm + G + M4 + S + M2 + LD + P + C = \text{illegal drug problem}$$

Mm is the moneymen who front the cash for the whole shebang. G is for the growers of the poppy, ganja, etc. M4 is for the 4-legged mules, horses, etc. that carry the product down the mountains or out of the valleys to the labs. S is for the scientists/experts who convert the product to heroin, cocaine, etc. M2 is for the 2-legged mules who carry the finished product to the local distributors. LD is for the, uh, local distributors. P is for the pushers on the streets, and if you'll pardon my French, I just have to say God damn The Pusherman, even though it ain't all his fault. To me, this is the only instance where this expletive is acceptable.

And now we get to the final variable. C is for the customer.

I also figured out (on my very own) that if we could just neutralize, eliminate, or simply remove just one (1) single variable – but it has to be the right one – in this equation, the illegal drug trade would cease to exist tomorrow.

That's right. The C. The customer. All the other variables can and would be replaced tomorrow if they disappeared today. Not the C. The C can't be replaced. If today everyone decided that they would do whatever it takes to get clean and never look back at the shit, the rest of it would fall apart tomorrow.

I think we have about 3 chances in 8 billion for that to happen. Now we're back to individuals making good choices.

There were many times I got so high that I was afraid I would never make it back, but I did. There are times now, though, that I wonder if I made it all the way back.

Say what you want about this one drinking because one of the parents was an alcoholic and the reason this one snorts cocaine is because that's how all those around him amuse themselves. But that person there at ground zero, the one about to turn up that bottle of Wild Turkey or the one leaning over that mirror on the table with a straw up his nose *still* has a chance to make a better decision.

I made a lot of bad decisions. I realize that now, but I can't go back. There is no going back. There is only now, and five minutes from now, and tomorrow, and forever.

These days, I try to teach my athletes to always think first and make the right decision. At any position on the baseball field, you have to know what you are going to do with the ball if it's hit to you, depending on how it's hit and where it's hit, *before* it's hit. A successful player knows the situation *before* the pitch is made: the score, how many outs, where the runners are on the bases, and thinks this through *before* every pitch. It only stands to reason that the same is true in life. Get prepared. No! *Stay* prepared!

Rest assured, at some point, someone is going to ask you to drink this, smoke that, or snort something else. Preparation is the only defense. The right thing to do is not always clear and it's not always easy, but deep down, the right decision is always at your disposal and it's never too late to make it.

Decisions, decisions, decisions...

deleted Chapter 14

CAREY AND I started our sophomore year hanging out on his family's farm, spending every weekend in a little shack across the road from his house. He always managed to get us a couple of fifths of Boone's Farm wine from somewhere and copious bags of munchies from his father's county store. He never took any wine from his dad's store because he knew C.D. Strickland kept a close watch on the alcohol inventory. We'd drink, laugh, tell lies, drink some more, and then puke our guts out and fall asleep. By Christmas, we'd moved on to smoking dope, munching black beauties (a type of speed) and drinking Schlitz Malt Liquor and Canadian Mist, which was a lot more fun and about the same amount of laughing and throwing up, but now we were able to stay awake and tell lies all night long.

Although we were well aware of the dangers, there was no way in the world to derail that *Hell-bound Train* once we'd boarded.

Please remain stoned until the ride comes to a complete stop.

We loved to get high and go to the late show at the Cardinal Theatre in Raleigh. Andy Warhol's *Trash* and Mad Dogs and Englishmen with Joe Cocker and friends were a couple of our favorites. Leon Russell, wow. We got tossed out of the theater one night, but we learned a valuable lesson: don't take acid and think you're going to get through the first ten minutes of Yellow Submarine. It can't be done.

Another habit we developed was analyzing the movie 'Reefer Madness' which played at the Cardinal just about every other weekend. This movie was the quintessential caveat about the insanity of marijuana and we'd crack up every single time we saw it. Even without a buzz, that movie is funny as hell, but in a certain way, it's also right on the money. They were wrong about smoking pot making people go apeshit and start killing people, but marijuana did (and always will), in its own devious and indiscernible little ways, open the doors to other illicit and enticing gateways leading to the Stairway to Heaven. Much more could be said and written about those other gateways and stairways but this is neither the time nor the place.

During our junior and senior years, we spent a lot of nights in Raleigh trying to wash out the bad taste of yet another defeat on the diamond by seeing how many pitchers of beer we could drink. At Darryl's Restaurant on Hillsborough Street across from North Carolina State University and at the Player's Retreat (The PR) around the corner on Oberlin Road, we became seasoned drinkers. We made a lot of friends there who opened our eyes to a whole lot of different substances to create and enhance a buzz. In our weak little minds, we justified it all by believing that we were just trying to take the rough edge off a long string of shitty baseball games. It's easy to fool yourself at seventeen.

The only good thing about having three different baseball coaches three years in a row is that we got to use the same trick three years running. Around lunchtime before every game – home or away – I would conveniently discover that I'd forgotten to pack my socks, or glove, or spikes, or whatever, and Carey would have to take me home to retrieve the wayward jockstrap because I didn't have a car. We'd smoke a joint or hit the hash pipe and then come back and play nearly perfect baseball.

I wish someone would explain to me how Carey and I could compete *almost* flawlessly, stoned to the bone, while most of the other guys, sober as preachers, couldn't pick up a weak grounder and throw somebody out at first base or catch a lazy fly ball in the outfield. I still can't understand it. Those guys were damn good baseball players!

I say 'almost flawlessly' but Carey and I did shit the bed – that's a figure of speech – one day and lost a close game all on our own. Talk about a biggie.

Tied 1-1 with Clayton in Clayton in the bottom of the 7th with two down and they had a runner at third. I don't know what anyone else was thinking, but a bunt with two outs was not even on my radar.

But that's what the batter did.

He laid down a perfect bunt up the 3rd baseline toward Carey and even though neither of us was expecting it, we were both on it in time to throw the guy out at first.

Carey and I both said, "I got it," at exactly the same time. Carey and I both heard each other say "I got it" at exactly the same time. Carey and I both stopped dead in our tracks at exactly the same time. You see where this is heading? Then Carey and I both tried to grab the ball at exactly the same time and neither one of us could find the damn handle on it. It was like a little greased white pig jumping around in the dirt. Game over.

The word 'embarrassed' doesn't even touch it. It took us about six pitchers of beer to drown that one.

Sometimes I think it's me. I'm just plain old bad luck.

Carey and I did, however, screw up badly one day during our senior year. We decided to 'trip' after lunch and just skip baseball practice that afternoon. We had abused LSD many times before, so we really didn't think much of it. I mean, it wasn't like we were in contention for the conference championship or anything at 0-11. What the hell? Who cares? It's just practice.

I feel certain that Jimi Hendrix was not being at all straightforward when he said he was simply relating a dream when he wrote *Purple Haze*. That shit is for real. Think: Lucy in the Sky with Diamonds…

After school, Carey drove us to one of our favorite hangouts – the Dairy Bar – which today we noticed had plasticine porters and damned if they weren't wearing looking-glass ties! Four more hoodlums, and I mean that in a loving way, poured into Carey's red Plymouth Road Runner. We blasted off for the guinea trails that ran haphazardly through the woods behind Wakelon, the old high school. Funny, I'd never noticed all the tangerine trees and today it was slightly overcast with marmalade skies.

After burning and hacking our way through six joints of what tasted like harsh stems and seeds that somebody had stashed at the base of a tree, we decided to go to Darryl's in Raleigh to see if we could drink them out of beer. On the way out of the magic forest, we encountered some rocking horse people and, believe it or not, they were eating marshmallow pies.

We hit the hardtop and two miles outside of Zebulon, who do we meet on the highway heading back into town? Hint: It wasn't that girl with the colorful kaleidoscope eyes. It was our baseball coach, Charles Corbett. He was pointing back toward town and if I'm not mistaken, and again I'm not, he was not happy. I guess it's not true that everyone has to smile as they drift past the pretty flowers.

I did.

We dumped the other four freaks back at the Dairy Bar, much to their bloodshot-eyed chagrin. Carey and I didn't discuss how totally messed up we were and what a very bad idea it was to go to baseball practice under the influence of LSD and smelling very much like Bob Marley's ass.

When we arrived in the parking lot, Carey said, "Be cool."

And I parroted, "Be cool." But I was thinking, *Oh, shit. Oh, shit. Oh, shit!*

Being cool simply meant keeping your shit together during stormy times. This was easy to do most of the time, but with strychnine in our bloodstream running around unsnapping all the synapses in our brains made being cool a little tougher than usual, for me anyway.

Our regular first baseman Anthony Brown was on the disabled list so I had to fill in at first during infield practice. Oh, goodie. Normally, I didn't do much of anything at practice except run because my arm was always killing me from pitching every game. Nothing was normal about this practice with all these green and yellow cellophane flowers growing inside my head.

Taking infield turned out to be a very interesting, uh, trip. Let's just say that I lucked up when I chose to field and catch the middle of the three multi-colored balls coming at me every time. I guess you'd call that triple vision, though I've never heard of it. The mental image in my recollection of that day is from the perspective of someone tall standing behind me, looking over my shoulder, and yes, maybe towering over my head, as opposed to seeing it happen through my own eyes.

Over on the other corner, the 'hot' corner, Carey was knocking down, stabbing, smothering, and eating up everything Coach Corbett was drilling down to third base. I swear, a few of the times Carey wasn't even looking at the ball being hit to him – he was looking over to first base at me with that ever-present, shit-eating grin of his.

Coach Corbett seemed to be getting madder and madder and I was worried that he might run us to death. By then I was seeing newspapers and taxis, but nothing appeared on the shore. I guess Coach got tired of fighting it and just laughed at us.

He *did* lose his shit, though, a few minutes later when we were throwing the ball around the horn and it somehow (maybe I threw it out there, who knows?) got into the outfield and *they* were throwing it around.

I acquired one of my most prominent and permanent idiot scars later during batting practice. Coach Corbett was throwing BP and after I had my turn at the plate, he told me run out my last swing and stay on first base. I say last 'swing' because I sure as hell wasn't getting any wood on the ball. I felt like I was trying to hit a wasp with a light pole.

Over at first, I got my little lead, even though I didn't really know what the hell I was doing, and Coach took his stretch. He looked over at me out of the corner of his left eye and then I saw him look back at the catcher.

For reasons I still don't understand, I took off like the proverbial bat out of hell toward second base. Out of the corner of *my* left eye, I watched Coach calmly step off the back of the pitching rubber and toss the ball to Mushroom standing on second. The throw went a little high and Mush had to leap into the air to catch it. I then leaped into the most beautifully executed head-first slide I've ever made. Perfect. I nailed that sucker. A perfect '10'! Textbook. The only problem was that I'd stopped sliding about three feet short of second base.

Seems I was having a little perception problem.

As I was lying there, examining the blood pooling and leaking from the large strawberry there on the inside of my right forearm, Mushroom walked over and slapped me on the head with the ball in his glove and said, "Yer out." Then he leaned down and whispered, "That'll teach ya to trip without me!"

Amid all the colors and exploding stars I was now seeing, Mush's "yer out" echoed hollowly a few times, too. *Nice effect*, I thought. After the colors faded, I looked around at Coach Corbett and saw all the other guys, including Carey, just shaking their heads.

Well, excuse me, while I kiss Lucy in the Sky with Diamonds!

There are a couple of other little 'stories within the game' from my high school baseball days that I just have to share and then I'll quit. I promise.

Mushroom, our second baseman and fellow head, had a spry, wiry old grandfather who came to see us play twice during my sophomore year. He was a very nice man, a cultured Southern gentleman, who stood about five-feet nothing, loved baseball, always dressed up in a dark three-piece suit, starched white shirt, and a red string tie. He had sparkling blue eyes behind some Buddy Holly black frame glasses and in his gnarled right hand he carried an equally gnarled but highly polished driftwood walking cane. One of the guys said he looked like a leprechaun, but he sure as hell didn't say it loud enough for Mushroom to hear it.

The two games that Mr. Robert Phillips came to see us play my sophomore year were the only two games we won. I didn't think much about it until my junior year, when he made it to only one of our games; the only game we won. Strange? Coincidence? Whatever. We were already devising plans to get him there for all of our games the following year.

Sometime during the winter of 1972, though, Mr. Phillips' health took a turn for the worse and he was unable to attend a single game my senior year. Don't bother looking back to see what my (our) record was that year. I'll save you the trouble: It was 0-14.

I sure could have used some more of that good luck.

Back during my tenth grade year, our regular catcher, Tim Draughon, got caught smoking a cigarette during school the day of our first conference game of the season. Naturally, Coach Jimmy Harris immediately removed Tim from the team, and rightfully so, except we didn't have another catcher. That afternoon, my new catcher was none other than the 5'4", 123-pound, freshman Guilford Edwards. I don't know if he volunteered to catch, or if he just didn't step back quickly enough with the other players when Coach Harris asked, "Who else can catch?"

The poor kid totally disappeared when he donned all the catcher's equipment. There was absolutely nothing left of Guilford, just a neat stack of catcher's gear. I think all the equipment weighed more than he did.

We were playing Franklinton at home so, in the top of the first inning, I was on the mound. I looked around at the three guys on base, all three of whom I'd just struck out. I thought to myself, *Ain't this some shit?* The guys on base were batters four, five, and six. I'd struck out one, two, and three as well, but they'd already scored. I looked in at the seventh batter of the inning. We had no outs and the score was three-zip. None of these guys have even come close to touching the ball with the bat.

Guilford was having no better luck trying to catch the wicked curveball I was slinging that day. It was breaking the full width of home plate and diving a good foot and a half through the strike zone. He's missed every pitch I've thrown, but how was he supposed to catch the ball with all that over-sized gear weighing him down and hampering his movement?

The umpire was pissed about getting beaten to death by the baseball *and* about how long it might take to finish this game. Guilford hadn't even come close to throwing anybody out stealing or at first base after all the missed third strikes. Again, how could he? I was thinking to myself this must be some kind of record for strikeouts in an inning, though I didn't really see it as a source of pride.

By the top of the 3rd inning, Gilford got it figured out. Instead of trying to catch the breaking ball cleanly, he just blocked it and smothered it right there behind home plate. I don't remember how the rest of the game went, but we only lost 7-6, so we at least made a decent showing. Gilford did eventually put on some size and became a very good baseball player later on. He was best known, however, for being a fearless pole-vaulter in his backyard.

I sure hope Guilford remembers that game the same way I do. He looked really healthy the last time I saw him.

The weirdness from the #2 position cropped up again the following year. Early in the season during my junior year, we were playing Fuquay-Varina at their place when another stranger-than-life thing happened. It was the bottom of the last inning, two outs, the score was tied at 2-2, and they had a guy on first. We had a chance to win this one.

The storm that had been threatening all afternoon suddenly stopped its threatening and began throwing lightning all over the place. It was quickly determined that we would finish this game when F-V came to visit us in a couple of weeks.

Baseball.... now-style

This is the new-style of baseball. Today's athletes sport long hair, (as does Allen White, pitcher for the Zebulon Cougars), and mustaches. Most of the Zebulon High School baseballers have flowing locks . . . but mustaches and long sideburns are obviously absent.

At home two weeks later, we resumed the postponed game just as it was when the storm hit: bottom of the seventh, two outs, runner on first, score 2-2. I'm not going to say that I had some kind of weird dream or premonition about how this game would end, but it ended much the way I feared it would. It was like watching a train wreck in slow motion: you see it unfold before your eyes, but there's not one damn thing you can do to stop it. I wish it had turned out differently, but it's definitely now one of the many things I can look back on and laugh about. Perhaps the reader will, too.

My first pitch was a strike. My catcher at the time (who will remain nameless because he's a good friend and bigger than me) missed the ball and the runner on first stole second easily. With the count 0-1, I threw another curveball and got another strike. My catcher missed the ball again and the runner swiped third. Now the count is 0-2.

I thought about wasting a pitch eye-high to see if I could get the batter to chase one out of the zone, but I wanted the strikeout. Aside from that, a guy that pitches every game doesn't have a whole lot of pitches to waste.

So instead of purposely throwing the high one, I threw a serious over the top breaking ball (the twelve to six gem that I learned from the batter's box and the right arm of the Franklinton kid a week before) that drops off the table right at the back point of home plate. The batter swung feebly at strike three, but my catcher missed the ball yet again.

To his credit, he scrambled to the ball quickly and wheeled around to throw out the batter going to first. He had plenty of time because the ball had careened off the backstop and rolled back to him. I was at the plate covering home, freezing the runner from 3rd base. But before he let it rip, in his peripheral vision, my catcher noticed the runner from third was standing halfway down the line and he kind of double-clutched his throw. I think my catcher had his left eye on the runner from third and his right eye on the guy going to first because he threw an absolute laser about twenty-five feet to the left of first base that rolled all the way to the fence in right center. The guy from third walked in, laughing his ass off, to score the winning run.

Three pitches, all strikes, and I lost the ballgame on a walk-off strikeout, E-2. That was the first time I ever really wanted to hit somebody in the head with my less-than-mediocre fastball and I was ashamed to admit that it was my very own catcher that I wanted to plunk.

My one claim to fame is that during my senior year, one of the coaches at Zebulon High School whispered to me one day that Clyde King, the legendary scout of the New York Yankees was coming to see me play at some point during the season. Was that true? I have no idea, but like I said, that's still my one claim to fame, whether true or not, and I'm sticking to it. Yes, that is a mighty thin claim. I never saw or heard from Mr. King if he did in fact scout me.

There was a little rumor on the team that Mr. King was in the stands one Saturday morning when we had to play a make-up game at home that had been rained out. I had just gotten home at about four a.m. and I'd already pitched three games that week: Monday, Tuesday and Thursday, and my arm was a wreck. My wrist and hand were partially numb, my elbow was screaming bloody murder, and my shoulder hurt like an abscessed tooth. Back then, there were no pitch counts or a limit on innings for pitchers, not that we were aware of, anyway. I know we lost the game and I certainly don't remember dominating it, that's for damn sure, but there is one thing I remember clearly.

The first batter of the game hit a looping, lazy pop fly back between first base, second base, and right field. First baseman Anthony Brown, second baseman Mushroom Phillips, and right fielder Doug Dunn got on their horses and took off wide-assed open after it. All three guys hit top speed right at the intersection where the ball dropped between them.

By the loving grace of God, they all crossed paths and just kept going in different directions. I would have been witness to the worst collision in baseball history and I'd have seen it up close and personal.

Apparently, the lead-off hitter had wheels because he was already rounding first as I was getting there to cover. My guys didn't bother to look back to see if anyone had caught the ball, so I had to sprint about fifty feet out to it. By the time I picked up the ball, the batter was rounding second base and was heading hard for third. Boy, he *did* have some wheels, didn't he? I had no time to plant my foot for the throw; I just turned and flicked it sidearm as hard as I could toward third base.

The throw had a lot of bend in it, but it was on the mark, bouncing once right into Carey's glove. He put the glove down and the guy slid into it about a foot in front of third base. Sweet.

Except the umpire called him 'safe' and I kind of lost it.

How the hell could the umpire blow such an easy call? Even worse than the call, I couldn't really say anything to him, either. The umpire was Amby Foote, my American Legion baseball coach and a former minor league pitcher back in the 1950s. At that point, I went inside myself and basically pouted for the rest of the game.

The bottom line? God gave me some serious natural athletic ability for baseball. I could pitch and hit, and I could play anywhere on the field a lefthander could play. I had the desire to play at the next level. I had coaches, teachers, friends, and family who believed in me.

What I didn't have, unfortunately, was one damn lick of sense.

deleted Chapter 15

My HIGH SCHOOL YEARS crawled swiftly to an end and, by the grace of that same God, I survived. I had made far too many bad decisions and wrong choices during those four years. God Himself probably couldn't believe some of the stuff I did, but He helped me through it. My grandmother died in January of my senior year, and I moved in with my brother Mike and his wife Maggie for the remainder of the school year. After that, I was on my own. Normally, you'd think a teenager living on his own is a good thing, even a great thing, but for someone with my particular propensities, eh, not so much.

When I graduated from high school in June of 1973 I was expected to go to college, play baseball, get signed by the Yankees or somebody, and live happily ever after. I had the skills and I had people pulling for me. I mean, I hate to brag, and I won't, because Cassius Clay said, "If you can do it, it ain't braggin'," and at the time, I could do it.

But then, more shit happens.

By the middle of October of 1973, I had flunked out of Louisburg College. During the summer, Coach Corbett had gone to bat for me, talking LC head coach Russ Frazier into giving me a grant-in-aid to play baseball. I went to classes the first three days and thought, *Man, this shit ain't for me.* I stayed and partied through the middle of October, though, just to be on the safe side.

After a long, wild night tripping with my roommate and some other guys on the hall, I figured it was time for me to bug out. I took off hitchhiking the next morning toward my old homeplace in Van, West Virginia and got there late the next evening. Two nights later on Friday, October 19, I was cruising around on curvy mountain roads with three of my friends.

We were all partying hard and trying to push it to the limit. We succeeded. Somehow, we managed to clip a telephone pole just before hitting a concrete bridge doing about 80 miles per hour. The friend sitting behind me in the right rear passenger seat, Ray James, was killed instantly. The rest of us were injured, but nothing serious. None of us would ever get over the mental wounds, though.

Rest in peace, Ray.

If I could get just one do-over of any day in my life, that would be the day.

By the end of December, I was back home and driving a truck for a local food distributor and staying lost in the damn ozone most of the time.

Bigtime failure on my part to realize that good intentions have to be backed up by some serious sacrifices. I just wasn't ready to grow up and abandon all the bad habits I had acquired during the past few years. In retrospect, I'm able to see some of God's plan more clearly. If I had been given a $25,000 signing bonus by some major league team, standard at the time, I would have been dead (overdosed) by the end of the week and I would have probably taken four or five of my closest friends with me. And the team would have lost $25,000.

Twenty-five large? What would I have done with twenty-five grand?

I can clearly see myself concentrating hard, one eye closed for focus and the other squinting for fine-tuning, trying to screw the tap into the top of that third, maybe fourth, ice cold keg of Budweiser, while holding a 16-oz. clear plastic cup in my teeth. One of my comrades in crime is stumbling through the door with two bags of ice. He's wearing only one shoe and it's one of mine. There's a half a case of Jack Daniels Tennessee whiskey on the floor beside the table. Wonder where the other half went?

Just sitting there on top of that table are the meager remains of what had once been kilo of Acapulco Gold, three empty packs of EZ Wider rolling papers, and a huge turquoise bong shaped like the Starship Enterprise. A large and heavy amber glass ashtray overflows with a nest of big, short, fat, and ugly legless roaches.

Two more guys are 'asleep' on the couch in a comic, yet romantically compromising pose. I've already taken several pictures. Right there beside that dwindling pile of herb superb is a tennis ball-sized block of 85% pure Peruvian flake cocaine, several single-edged razor blades, a colorful assortment of straws of various lengths, a couple of rolled up hundred dollar bills, and an open box of Arm & Hammer baking soda.

Another friend is sitting Yoga-style under the table staring at his hands, moving them in circles every now and then to watch the trails. On one corner of the table, underneath the eight box-seat tickets to the next Yankees-Red Sox game and eight roundtrip plane tickets to the Big Apple, someone has tried to hide the Needle and the Spoon and our last trip to the moon without much success. And there's a kickass Kenwood stereo system in the middle of the floor with four refrigerator-sized speakers in each corner of the room, jarring the walls with Pink Floyd's *Money*. And you know what? It IS a hit. And I'd never try to give you any kind of that do-goody-good bullshit.

Two very fine young ladies have just sashayed into the room from skinny dipping in the pool. Where did I hide, I mean, where did I put their towels? Oh, yeah, and there's a flattened bag of Planter's peanuts under one of the rockers of the wicker chair. The peanuts are fine, but I don't like the dude with the monocle and cane. He scares me.

And that's just day one.

Twenty-five thousand dollars? You can't tell me that God hasn't been watching out for this old boy.

I stumbled through several more jobs between 1974 and 1976: carpenter, farm hand, commercial fisherman, and sports editor and ad layout for the local weekly newspaper.

Working at the Zebulon Record, the local weekly newspaper, was definitely my best gig. I learned how to lay out advertisements, among other things, working with a true graphic genius and great artist, Wayne Wilson. Somehow I allowed myself to get talked into writing a sports column every week. Apparently, I've *never* known how to say no. I'm glad I did it, though, because I received a lot of good comments on my column.

I was so simple-minded I just called it "Sports Stuff" and wrote about whatever I wanted. Instead of having my picture on the logo, Wayne had found a nice clip-art piece of a cartoon guy standing there holding every kind of sporting equipment you could think of. Sports Stuff. I got in free at all the local athletic events and even learned how to misuse a real camera and became proficient at screwing stuff up in the darkroom.

My most vivid memories of my time at the newspaper was sneaking off from work to the baseball field under the pretense of some kind of interview or another. Oh, I would do an interview, but there was never that much to it. Ten minutes and it was done. What I was really doing was pitching batting practice to the current high school team.

All that ended one afternoon when Stanley "No Show" Jones threw a frozen rope all the way from the outfield fence to the mound. The ball must have been about twenty feet away from me when Stanley yelled my name and I turned around to see what the hell he wanted.

Getting a fractured jaw during an interview can be explained away in many and varied ways, I guess, but too many people knew the real story, so I had to fess up to the truth. My boss, Ken Wilson, a great editorialist and photographer, wasn't bothered at all by my misfortune and actually thought it was kind of funny that Karma had bitten me in the, uh, ass so hard. I was supposed to be working for him but instead I was out pitching batting practice to the local high school team. Yeah, I guess it was funny watching me eat soup through a straw at lunch for three weeks. Good way to lose weight, though.

I suppose, like everything else in life, it all boils down to perspective.

The folks at the newspaper encouraged me to attend Chowan College to enhance my journalism skills, or more likely, just to get rid of me, so in January of 1976, I gave college another try.

At Chowan, I was practicing regularly with the baseball team and I was planning to try out for the football team as a punter, not a quarterback. A man has to know his limitations. I was doing well in all my classes and actually enjoying learning new things. A few years of maturity makes a lot of difference.

You'd think.

Getting caught smoking pot one night while studying in my dorm room was NOT in my plans, but it happened. In the middle of February, I was back in Zebulon, living with whichever friend that would have me for a few weeks. I worked a few more dead-end, non-descript jobs for nearly a year. There were some very lean times in between some of those jobs when I had no money, no place to live, and I ate very little. But somehow, probably with A Little Help From My Friends, I manage to stay high and get by.

In the summer of 1977, I started working in the auto parts business as a counterman and a salesman and then eventually into managing an auto parts warehouse. This I did from about 1977 through the end of 1990.

Exciting, huh? Oh, you should have been there.

Options were few in the mid to late-seventies for a guy wanting to play baseball if he's in his twenties and not in college or the pros. As a matter of fact, I may have miscounted. There was only *one* other option: the last remnants of the old Negro Leagues, which were by then just barnstorming teams hooking up for a weekend of baseball.

Now, I don't know if you noticed from the pictures or not, but I'm as about as white as a person can get, all the way down to my last name. Like I said earlier, I was a little naïve about the whole black/white thing here in the South and it didn't bother me one damn bit. I just wanted to play ball.

My right fielder and very good friend, Doug Dunn, who is black, played on his father's team that barnstormed around here in the Carolinas and Virginia during the summer months. Doug and I were (and still are) like brothers and his mother and father treated me like a son, adding some soul to my already unconventional family dynamic. Now wouldn't that be a nice family portrait hanging over the fireplace? Yes. Yes, it would.

Doug's dad Willie invited me to play with them several times and I enjoyed it immensely. I performed well most of the time, but I met several guys who were tremendous baseball players and I may have been a bit intimidated. The catcher on our team, Speedro, was my dream catcher. Nothing got by him. Even if I broke off a curveball a foot in front of home plate, he was on it like white on rice. Maybe that's not a good comparison, but you know what I mean. He was a very demanding catcher, too.

If I was having trouble locating my pitches where he wanted them, he would throw the ball back to me about *twice as hard as I was throwing it in.* That was very embarrassing, but it did help me kick my game up a notch or two.

I kind of lost interest in that team (or they lost interest in me) after a few summers and I started playing softball. I'd always thought of softball as a sport for girls, but that's what all the other guys were doing those days, and hey, you take what you can get, right?

Playing softball was surely a step down from baseball, but I had to play something, for goodness sake, I was still a kid! In 1982, when I started dating Pam, my future wife, I was playing some serious softball for three different teams during the week. That was at least one, if not two, and many times three games every night, not to mention a travel team that played tournaments on the weekends. The tournament team's roster included my buddy Welton Pearce, who also played on two of the other three teams with me. Me and Gomez was tight if you know what I mean. Worm was a man of many nicknames.

If you didn't happen to get one, I know where it went.

In the subdued game of softball, and I'm talking slow-pitch here, the mound wasn't the place to be. You could get your ass killed there. I played first base some, but mainly I could be found roaming the sweet green acres of left field. My arm was pretty much shot by then, but I really loved playing defense. My big old outfielder's glove sucked up base hits, fly balls, line drives and anything else anyone cared to hit my way.

Playing the outfield is pretty simple: you just run it down, keep it in front of you, and get the ball back to the infield. That old glove of mine never made a single error the whole time I played. Now, *I* made one every blue moon or two, but the glove? The glove was perfect.

It's really unfair how easy it is to hit in softball. The only difficult part of it is keeping your discipline at the plate and NOT trying to hit it over an outfielder's head and just making a long out. I still hit it as hard as I could, I just had to wait and let it get by me a little, and then rip it to the opposite field over third or short and be on second base by the time the ball got back to the infield. With the bases only 60 feet apart, it was rarely a challenge. Even if I got under it too much, most of the time it had such a nasty slice the left fielders usually misplayed it.

One of the best compliments I ever received was from a kid named Ken Griswold. (That kid now has two grown children of his own.) I'd made it to the field in Zebulon just in time for our nine o'clock game. With two games already under my belt that evening, I was loose as a goose and ready to rumble. I went 5 for 5 that night and as we were shaking hands with the other team at the end of the game, Ken said, "What are you batting now, Allen? Seven-fifty?" I didn't really keep up with my stats in softball, but I was actually a little dismayed because I thought I was batting closer to .875, maybe even .900 or better. With discipline, anyone can get a clean base hit nine out of ten times at bat in softball. If you couldn't, you shouldn't be playing.

When Pam and I were married on June 13 of 1983, I was still playing for four different softball teams. By the time Jameson was born October 16, 1984, I'd cut down to two teams. A year later, I was playing only for my church team, when I could make it. Talk about getting sent down to the minors! When Taylor was born August 16, 1988, I hadn't played any kind of ball in nearly a year.

I had coached recreation league baseball and been an assistant coach with the Pee Wee and Mighty Mite football teams since I was 21. In 1988, I became head coach of the Mighty Mites when long-time friend and head coach Keith Temple retired. It was obvious to everyone but me that this football coaching thing was now taking up way too much of my time.

I hate to admit it, but I could halfway see Pam's point on this one. It was bad enough that we practiced every day of the week and we (the guys on my coaching staff) were getting together for a few hours on Sunday afternoons to go over the video from Saturday night's game action. We're still talking Pee Wee and Mighty Mite football here, folks.

All that was bad enough, but when we visited the town of Clayton for a game one Saturday and I saw their coaching staff walking around with headsets wired to some other coaches up in the press box, I had a feeling that midget football had just gone a little too far. After a few more weeks, it all became too much and I resigned in the middle of the season. Letting football go gave me more energy to devote to my full time job during the week and a part-time job on the weekends.

At this point, the deleted Chapter 15 connected with the old Chapter 16, but this little piece of autobiography derailed the story. The gap it created between the first and second half of the real story was just too wide. I thought I was doing the right thing, but now here I am with no ending at all…